Beyond *the* Honeymoon

OTHER BOOKS AND AUDIOBOOKS

MARK D. OGLETREE

The Making of a Man
Babysitters Are Cheaper than Divorces
So You're in Love, Now What?
Finding Peace in Difficult Times
Presidents of the Church
Preparing for Your Celestial Marriage
Just Married
No Other Success
First Comes Love Then Comes Marriage
Courageous Parenting
By Divine Design
Raising an Army of Helaman's Warriors

DOUGLAS E. BRINLEY

Between Husband and Wife
Eternal Families
America's Hope
Behold the Lamb of God
Strengthening Your Marriage and Family
Toward a Celestial Marriage

25 QUESTIONS AND ANSWERS
ABOUT MARITAL INTIMACY

Beyond *the* Honeymoon

Mark D. Ogletree, Kinsey D. Pistorius,
and Douglas E. Brinley

Cover image *Young couple sitting in sand on beach* © by ronstik / Adobe Stock

Cover design copyright © 2024 by Covenant Communications, Inc.

Published by Covenant Communications, Inc.
American Fork, Utah

Copyright © 2024 by Mark D. Ogletree, Kinsey D. Pistorius, Douglas E. Brinley
All rights reserved. No part of this book may be reproduced in any format or in any medium without the written permission of the publisher, Covenant Communications, Inc., PO Box 416, American Fork, UT 84003. This work is not an official publication of The Church of Jesus Christ of Latter-day Saints. The views expressed within this work are the sole responsibility of the author and do not necessarily reflect the position of The Church of Jesus Christ of Latter-day Saints, Covenant Communications, Inc., or any other entity.

Printed in the United States of America
First Printing: March 2024

30 29 28 27 26 25 24   10 9 8 7 6 5 4 3 2 1

Table of Contents

Introduction: *1*

Question 1: *5*
I am about to get married. My parents have never talked to me about sex. Should I ask my parents to give me the sex talk?

Question 2: *9*
How can you know your sexual compatibility before marriage if you live the law of chastity?

Question 3: *15*
What kinds of affection are appropriate prior to marriage?

Question 4: *21*
What should couples talk about before marriage, especially regarding physical intimacy?

Question 5: *31*
What if you are fairly naïve and don't know what to do the first time you have sex?

Question 6: *37*
What if you feel anxious or scared about having sex?

Question 7: *43*
Now that we are engaged, how can we best prepare for intimacy?

Question 8: *49*
How should a couple prepare and plan for the honeymoon?

Question 9: *55*
What do I need to know about birth control?

Question 10: *61*
What if you had sex prior to marriage with someone else? Should you reveal this to your partner?

Question 11: *67*
Is there any advice you could give to those of us who have a fiancé(e) who has been a victim of sexual molestation/abuse?

Question 12: *73*
What if you know you cannot have children? When should you tell your fiancé(e)?

Question 13: *79*
What are some ways for couples to talk about their sexual relationship? How often should those conversations take place?

Question 14: *89*
How often should couples be intimate?

Question 15: *95*
Does the Church have an official stance on what sexual acts are appropriate within marriage? Are there guidelines on what couples can "do" and "not" do?

Question 16: *101*
If sexual problems are one of the leading causes of divorce, what are some common marital intimacy problems?

Question 17: *109*
What do you do when you want to have sex and your spouse does not?

Question 18: *117*
   Is it selfish to tell your spouse no to sex?

Question 19: *125*
   What if I want to be intimate more often than my husband does? Is that bad?

Question 20: *131*
   What if sex is painful or difficult for the woman?

Question 21: *135*
   What if your spouse thinks sex is evil?

Question 22: *143*
   What if pornography has been a problem for your fiancé(e) or spouse?

Question 23: *157*
   How do you get over the feeling that all your husband wants to do is have sex?

Question 24: *165*
   How does having children change the sexual relationship between husband and wife?

Question 25: *173*
   What can married couples do to keep their love alive?

Conclusion: *182*

Introduction

"Your love, like a flower, must be nourished."
—President Spencer W. Kimball[1]

BACK IN 2000, DR. DOUGLAS Brinley and Dr. Stephen Lamb published the book *Between Husband and Wife: Gospel Perspectives on Marital Intimacy.* This wonderful book was one of the first of its kind—a book on marital intimacy written by two faithful Latter-day Saints. In *Between Husband and Wife*, the authors looked at intimacy from a medical, emotional, physical, and spiritual perspective. Doug and Stephen wanted to help couples prepare for their honeymoon and then, following the initial venture into sexual relations, provide information to assist couples in making any needed adjustments over their lifetime as intimate partners.

The book was a huge success and has been through several printings. We believe that the book's success points to a need among members of The Church of Jesus Christ of Latter-day Saints to have more resources available to help them navigate their way through this sacred, personal, and intimate adventure. However, *Between Husband and Wife* was published over twenty years ago, and since then, the world has changed drastically, and we sensed the need for a book that would speak to the current generation. We also know that sexual intimacy is a sensitive area to address and felt that contemporary couples need tools, principles, and advice from clinicians and other experts to help them navigate their way through this sacred part of marriage.

Consequently, Mark teamed up with his mentor, Doug Brinley, and his good friend and colleague Kinsey Pistorius to write this book. Doug brings a wealth of knowledge to this subject, having written on intimacy before. Doug

---

1 Spencer W. Kimball, *Faith Precedes the Miracle* (1972), 130–131.

has also written many other books on marriage and family-related topics and is a retired religion professor from Brigham Young University.

Kinsey also brings a deep perspective to marriage and family relationships. She has a PhD in marriage and family therapy, supervises other therapists in this area of work, and started her career working with families around sexual trauma. Kinsey has counseled young adults and couples for over twenty years and currently works in private practice in the Dallas, Texas area. Because of Kinsey's research and clinical experience in the field of marital therapy, her voice is critical to our book.

Mark is an associate professor in the religion department at Brigham Young University, has been in private practice for over thirty years, and has written numerous books and articles on marriage and family issues. Along with his wife, Janie, Mark directs a podcast called *Preserving Families*. Mark also provides weekly content to the podcast *Stand by My Servants*. This program is focused on the living prophets, their lives, and their teachings.

Both Doug and Mark have taught LDS college students, collectively, over the past six decades. Some of that teaching occurred at LDS Institutes of Religion, but most of it took place at Brigham Young University. Each semester over the course of these many years, they have taught classes on marriage and family relationships. Part of the curriculum for the courses they have taught on marriage and family has included sections on sexual intimacy. Perhaps surprising to some, their students have had more questions about the sexual relationship than any other gospel-related topic.

Mark wanted his students to feel comfortable asking questions about sexual relationships in marriage, so several years ago, he began the practice of inviting his students to text their questions to him. Since he did not have any of the students' cell phone numbers in his phone, this practice became an anonymous way to collect questions over the past several years. This exercise gave students the freedom to ask questions that they would never be comfortable asking in class.

Therefore, over the years, we have collected hundreds of questions on intimacy. Although we knew that we could not address every question (the book would fill volumes), we chose twenty-five of the most commonly asked questions and commenced our work articulating gospel-centered responses to the best of our combined abilities.

Since we understand that every person is unique, we decided that the most effective method in responding to the questions would be to identify principles—particularly gospel principles—that could help address each inquiry, while providing additional practical and clinical applications.

Elder David A. Bednar taught that gospel principles are "doctrinally based guideline[s] for the righteous exercise of moral agency. Principles . . . provide direction."[2] Elder Richard G. Scott added that "principles are concentrated truth, packaged for application to a wide variety of circumstances."[3] Since every couple is unique, each individual will have different attitudes, beliefs, and experiences that will require personal adaptation as issues emerge in their relationship.

Our knowledge base comes from our own lives and personal experiences, our counseling caseload, clinical trainings and research, experiences that our students have shared with us, ecclesiastical experiences, and the teachings and principles that are found in the scriptures and the words of latter-day prophets.

Marriage: The Roughest Contact Sport

The late Dr. Carlfred Broderick, a marriage and family therapist, psychologist, author, and professor at the University of Southern California, once wrote, "The most popular—and the roughest—contact sport in the country is not professional football; it is marriage."[4] Perhaps one of the reasons marriage fits that description is due to the level of intimacy marriage offers.

Unhealthy sexual relationships and challenges with intimacy can often lead to significant difficulties and unhappiness in marriage. One of the purposes of this book is to address potential sexual challenges in marriage and how to overcome them—especially for Latter-day Saint newlyweds. Another purpose of this book is to provide couples access to the tools, skills, principles, and practices that will assist them in having happy and fulfilling sexual lives together. We hope that this book will help readers discover answers to their questions and provide a comfortable venue (in your own home or apartment) for learning about sexual intimacy.

Another goal we had in writing this book was to answer the twenty-five questions in a succinct manner, using smaller page counts when possible, to provide key points, principles, explanations, and practical helps. The book is designed so that you do not need to read it in chronological order but can look up any question for further understanding, guidance, and practical suggestions. We hope you appreciate our approach on this sacred and sensitive topic.

---

2 David A. Bednar, "The Principles of My Gospel," *Ensign* or *Liahona*, May 2021.
3 Richard G. Scott, "Acquiring Spiritual Knowledge," *Ensign*, Nov. 1993, 86.
4 Carlfred Broderick, *Couples* (2014), 13.

Question #1
I am about to get married. My parents have never talked to me about sex. Should I ask my parents to give me the sex talk?

When it comes to the topic of sex, there's one common question we have all wondered about: How did you learn about sex? Whether it was through a conversation with your parents, reading a book, a friend mentioning the word, jokes made at school, or other various ways, we all know when we first learned what sex was. You may reflect on whether it was a positive or a negative experience, where you were, and who was involved in the conversation. Not only was that first "sex talk" important, but even more important to consider is how did you continue to learn about sex? You see, learning about "the birds and the bees" is not a one-time experience but instead consists of many different types of incoming messages and information—this book being one of them! Mark likes to joke that he still has not received the sex talk from his parents, and he's now a grandfather. Many others have had similar experiences.

Right now, you are at a point in your life where you want to learn more about sex as you embark on marriage and engage in a sexual relationship with someone you love. Your parents may be a great resource for your questions. However, in some cases, adolescents and children know little about sexual relationships because their parents have never talked to them about this important and sensitive topic. In other instances, some children have been exposed to pornography or have overheard their peers talking about sexual ideas, scenarios, and perhaps even experiences. Too often, many of the things that children and youth hear about sex from their peers are incorrect, grossly exaggerated, or even discussed in negative tones. Loving parents could help their children understand sexual relationships in healthy ways and can open a dialogue for future discussions.

Principle
Prophets have clearly stated that parents have the responsibility to teach their children concerning the sacred nature of marital intimacy as they mature

and move toward marriage. President Harold B. Lee taught, "Most important in a home is to have a father who doesn't shirk his responsibility to his sons when they seek and need answers to delicate questions and he too takes time to answer them. . . . Parents, stay close to your children. You mothers, stay close to your daughters."[1]

Parents are to be their children's prime teachers—especially when it comes to religion, morals, and values.[2] In the Doctrine and Covenants, we read, "And again, inasmuch as parents have children in Zion, or in any of her stakes which are organized, that teach them not to understand the doctrine of repentance, faith in Christ the Son of the living God, and of baptism and the gift of the Holy Ghost by the laying on of hands, when eight years old, the sin be upon the heads of the parents."[3] In this section of scripture, parents are also commanded to teach their children to pray, to keep the Sabbath day holy, and to walk uprightly before the Lord. In the Book of Mormon, we learn that parents have a responsibility to teach their children to walk in the ways of truth and soberness.[4] The spirit of these verses would include teaching our children about chastity, fidelity, and sexual relationships.

Explanation

When we teach about intimacy in our Brigham Young University classes, we always ask our students how many of them have had the "sex talk" with their parents. What we have observed has been shocking. Less than one-third of our students claim that their parents have ever talked to them about sex. Even a smaller proportion of students have had a talk with their parents about sex prior to their wedding. Our friend and colleague Dr. Matthew O. Richardson wrote,

> Unfortunately, many parents may not be teaching their children about sexual issues as well as they could. For example, in surveying over 200 active young single Latter-day Saints, I found that only 15 percent considered their parents to be the primary source of information regarding sexual issues.

---

1 *The Teachings of Harold B. Lee*, ed. Clyde J. Williams (1996), 227.
2 Spencer W. Kimball taught that "The home is the teaching situation [for sex education]. Every father should talk to his son, every mother to her daughter. Then it would leave them totally without excuse should they ignore the counsel they have received" (*Teachings of Spencer W. Kimball* [1982], 342–343).
3 Doctrine and Covenants 68:25.
4 *See* Mosiah 4:15.

These young members said they learned about this important topic primarily from friends or peers, the Internet, media, entertainment, textbooks, extended family, or their Church leaders.[5]

Many Latter-day Saint parents could certainly improve in this area. One way or another, our children are going to learn about sex. It will be much better for children—even adult children—to learn about procreation from their parents rather than from movies, novels, music, or their sexually inexperienced friends. There is one place where children can and should learn the sanctity and sacredness of a sexual relationship, and that is from kind, wise, and loving parents.

Elder Mark E. Petersen offered some timeless counsel when he taught

> Sex education belongs in the home, where parents can teach chastity in a spiritual environment as they reveal the facts of life to their children. There, in all plainness, the youngsters can be taught that procreation is part of the creative work of God and that, therefore, the act of replenishing the earth must be kept on the high plane of personal purity that God provides, free from all forms of perversion.[6]

Usually, parents understand their children better than anyone else. Directed by the Spirit, well-meaning parents will know how much to tell their children about sexuality and when to tell them. Parents should be the best resource for sex education because they are often available to answer children's questions. Parents and children often share the same values and belief system. Along with teachings about sex, parents should also instruct their children about chastity, fidelity, pornography, and self-control. *Talking about the sexual relationship should be as natural and normal as discussing gospel principles.* We also recognize that not all children have parents that would be willing to talk about sexual relationships, and others simply do not have a mother, or father, or in some cases, either. We also recognize that not every parent will have a healthy view of the sexual relationship, and therefore, the counsel or help they offer may be warped to some degree. Hopefully, there is another family member, friend,

---

5 Matthew O. Richardson, "Teaching Chastity and Virtue," *Ensign* or *Liahona*, Oct. 2012, 20.
6 Mark E. Petersen, in Conference Report, Apr. 1969, 64.

Church leader, or mentor that could take you under their wing and have these discussions with you.

If children or adolescents are taught about sex from other peers, television, movies, or social media, they could grow up with a skewed view of the sexual relationship. For example, some movies teach teenagers that they should have sex daily and that women are sexual objects—not daughters of God. Some friends pass on distorted views about sex, including lies and exaggerations. Perhaps this is why President Ezra Taft Benson taught parents, "Encourage your children to come to you for counsel with their problems and questions by listening to them every day. Discuss with them such important matters as dating, sex, and other matters affecting their growth and development, and do it early enough so they will not obtain information from questionable sources."[7]

Our experiences have been positive with our own children—especially when they were older and could understand more. We have also treasured the talks with our children just prior to their wedding. In fact, those conversations were bonding experiences. Therefore, if your parents have not had the sex talk with you, invite them to do so. If you do not have a trustworthy parent you can talk to, seek the counsel of a wise friend, leader, mentor, or even sibling whom you trust.

Practical Application

Of course, your parents have the responsibility to teach you about this sacred part of marriage, but parents may not initiate that conversation with you. Therefore, we suggest that you approach them as you near your marriage date and ask them (or at least your same-sex parent) to help you prepare for this new relationship. It might sound like this: "Dad, as you know, I'm getting married soon, and I need your counsel on how to view/approach/prepare for the sexual part of marriage. What can I expect from this relationship? What can I look forward to? Help me to know how to treat my new wife." Likewise, a young bride-to-be might ask her mom, "Mom, I'm approaching my wedding and honeymoon, and I'm not sure what to expect. What counsel would you give me about the honeymoon and then beyond? What's your best advice for me?" Parents and children can enjoy this special time of private and personal communication. This should not be a one-time discussion, but something ongoing. There is richness, bonding, and deep connection that can come during these sacred discussions.

---

7 *Teachings of Ezra Taft Benson* (1988), 499.

Question #2:
How can you know your sexual compatibility before marriage if you live the law of chastity?

To be compatible is to exist in harmony with another person, or to be suitable, or right for each other. Compatible couples find that they get along well with each other, work well together, enjoy each other's company, like similar things, enjoy similar hobbies, and have a lot in common, including their beliefs and values. Compatibility does not imply that your relationship is problem free! Instead, compatibility implies that regardless of the conflicts and challenges you encounter, you will be able to work through them together as a team. Moreover, you will become unified in your values and beliefs and in the manner you live your life.

Prior to marriage, it may seem difficult to determine whether you are sexually compatible with someone if you are living the law of chastity. This is one reason why so many contemporary couples in our nation cohabitate prior to marriage; they feel it is the best way to determine their sexual compatibility. Unfortunately, relationships built merely on a sexual foundation do not always morph into high levels of marital satisfaction and happiness. Did you know that when compared to couples who cohabitate, married couples report higher sexual satisfaction?[1] Furthermore, did you know that most contemporary cohabitating relationships in our country do not transition into marriage?[2]

---

1   See S. Stroope, M. J. McFarland, & J. E. Uecker, "Marital characteristics and the sexual relationships of US older adults: An analysis of national social life, health, and aging project data," *Archives of Sexual Behavior*, 44 (2015), 233–247, doi:10.1007/s10508-014-0379-y; *see also* Waite, L. & Joyner, K., "Emotional satisfaction and physical pleasure in sexual unions: Time horizon, sexual behavior, and sexual exclusivity," *Journal of Marriage and Family* 63 (2001a), 247–264 doi:10.1111/j.1741-3737.2001.00247.x.

2   *See* C. Copen, K. Daniels & W. Mosher, "First Premarital Cohabitation in the United States: 2006–2010 National Survey of Family Growth," *National Health Statistics Reports* 64 (Apr. 4, 2013): 1–3.

Nevertheless, if someone is looking to build a long-term relationship solely on sexual compatibility, they will likely be disappointed in the end.

A middle-aged man shared with one of us the following experience. He said that during his junior year in high school, while traveling on a bus to a track meet, his coach decided to teach him and some of the other athletes a lesson on marriage. The coach said, "Make sure you live with someone for a while before you get married; that way you can know whether or not you are sexually compatible." Our friend who shared this experience said, "Although I wasn't a member of the Church at the time, as soon as I heard my coach's suggestion, I instantly knew it was wrong." Our friend further explained that he believed there was much more to marriage than merely the sexual relationship. "I guess if sex is the foundation you want to build your life on," he said, "then marrying someone you feel sexually compatible with makes sense, but as a sixteen-year-old young man, I knew in my heart that there was much more to marriage than just sex. I wanted to build my future on a foundation that would last a lifetime—and perhaps even longer." Several years later, this young man found The Church of Jesus Christ of Latter-day Saints, was baptized, served a wonderful mission, and married a beautiful young woman in the temple. Today, they are enjoying their large and loving family.

Since many faithful Latter-day Saints live the law of chastity, having a premarital sexual relationship is not an option for testing sexual compatibility. Satan would have us believe that premarital sex is a prerequisite for a happy and fulfilling married life. In actuality, this concept of chastity before marriage is not only a religious tenet; social scientists are discovering the benefits of this concept too. Research confirms that premarital cohabitation to "test sexual compatibility" actually increases the chances of divorce. Cohabiting partners lack a higher level of commitment and have lower standards of behavior for their partners compared to those who are married.[3] Several years ago, another study compared married couples to cohabitating couples across several variables. Ironically, the study found that couples who waited until they were married to have a sexual relationship reported that their sexual satisfaction was 15 percent better than couples who hit the honeymoon before they were married.[4]

---

3   See Paul R. Amato, "Research on Divorce: Continuing Trends and New Developments," *Journal of Marriage and Family* 72 (2010), 650–666.
4   See Bill Hendrick, "Benefits in Delaying Sex Until Marriage," *WEBMD Health News* (Dec. 28, 2010), https://www.oodegr.com/english/psyxotherap/benefits_delayed_sex.htm.

Principle

"Be one; and if ye are not one ye are not mine."[5] Speaking of marriage, Elder Spencer J. Condie explained, "Unity—emotional and spiritual, as well as physical—is absolutely essential to a happy marriage, one in which the partners symbolically become one in all things."[6] Certainly, one of the ultimate goals in marriage is to become unified—to become one in heart and soul and mind. Part of that oneness is the sexual union, where married couples can become as close physically and emotionally as two people can be. In healthy marriages, compatibility begins and is strengthened outside of the bedroom. As the lives of a husband and wife become deeply connected and intertwined, the sexual union can become a natural result of their compatibility. Elder Jeffrey R. Holland explained it this way:

> They work together, they cry together, they enjoy Brahms and Beethoven and breakfast together, they sacrifice and save and live together for all the abundance that such a totally intimate life provides such a couple. And the external symbol of that union, the physical manifestation of what is a far deeper spiritual and metaphysical bonding, is the physical blending that is part of—indeed, a most beautiful and gratifying expression of—that larger, more complete union of eternal purpose and promise.[7]

Explanation

Sexual compatibility suggests that couples will want physical intimacy in the same way, at the same time, and with the same frequency. Hence, the assumption is that such couples could attain marital happiness as long as they are both continually satisfied and fulfilled sexually. Yet very few couples have their hormones so in sync so that they always want to have sex at the exact same time. Furthermore, sexual compatibility would suggest that their preferences are the same or that they want to have sex the exact same way. Even fewer couples would agree on how often they should engage in sexual intimacy. God did not design all men and women with the same sexual needs and desires or their bodies to experience pleasure in the same exact ways. Instead, it is

---

5 Doctrine and Covenants 38:27.
6 Spencer J. Condie, "Finding Marital Unity," *Ensign*, July 1986, 52.
7 Jeffrey R. Holland, "Of Souls, Symbols, and Sacraments," (Brigham Young University devotional, Jan. 12, 1988), speeches.byu.edu.

important to acknowledge and respect similarities *and* differences between you and your partner in order to strengthen your sexual compatibility.

Current research indicates a person's beliefs about long-term relationships affect how they experience overall sexual satisfaction. Specifically, if a person maintains "destiny beliefs" in a relationship, they believe they have a soulmate or very few people with whom they would be compatible. This implies that if a husband and wife *do not* see eye to eye on sexual satisfaction or on sexual frequency, for example, they could end up believing that they married the wrong person or that their relationship is doomed for failure. Destiny believers are also more likely to place emphasis on sexual performance, report lower relationship quality, and report less overall sexual satisfaction. Conversely, people with "growth beliefs" in relationships believe that sexual satisfaction takes work to maintain and that challenges can be overcome. Growth believers accept that imperfections are part of a relationship and expect to weather the complications together. People who have growth beliefs regarding relationships report more connection during sex, a higher quality relationship, and an overall increased sexual satisfaction with their partner.

Thus, the idea that you must marry someone with whom you can have complete sexual unity is a huge myth. This concept is taught by the makers of Hollywood movies, found in romance novels, and perhaps found in magazines located next to the checkout counter in the grocery store. Like all aspects of marriage—such as developing good communication skills, putting your spouse first, learning to make sacrifices for each other, and raising children together—you will need to go to work on any possible sexual issues or challenges that arise as a team and learn to improve in these areas. More importantly, as you work on strengthening all aspects of your marriage, sexual compatibility will come.

To some degree, marrying someone we are sexually compatible with is perhaps placing the focus in the wrong area. We recognize that many LDS couples are preoccupied with getting married so they can have a healthy and happy sexual relationship. However, once these couples are married and the honeymoon phase is over, they come to realize that having sex in marriage is a very small part of daily living. Believe us—there are many other things that will fill your life and schedule once you are married. The broader vision of marriage includes employment, household chores, financial obligations, raising children, Church duties and responsibilities, and a host of other activities. Building a marriage primarily on sex makes for a weak foundation and will not deliver the happiness and bliss some couples might expect.

Practical Application

Sexual compatibility is something couples *create together* once they are married. Developing such compatibility is a process that may take some time to establish and can be continually improved upon. Couples can develop sexual compatibility by communicating about sex, trying to meet their partner's needs, giving and receiving feedback, and increasing emotional intimacy.

Couples can enrich their physical compatibility by communicating openly and honestly about sex. This includes expressing your own sexual needs and desires in a clear and healthy way with each other as well as what feels good physically and what does not. After all, a partner cannot know what is sexually enjoyable and what is not if their spouse does not communicate it to them. Revealing this information requires vulnerability and transparency for both partners. However, sharing with each other what you want to happen in the bedroom increases overall relationship satisfaction, even more than the amount of sex you are having. In addition, a husband or wife cannot work on any issues or concerns if their spouse does not open up and discuss these issues specifically. Therefore, communication is paramount if couples want to increase their sexual compatibility. Marriage and family expert Michele Weiner Davis explained:

> We have this crazy notion that our spouses are just supposed to know what pleases us. We shouldn't have to talk about having good sex; it should just happen. But good sex doesn't just happen. Since no two people are alike, no single formula works for everybody. What one person finds arousing and exciting is a pure turn-off to another. If you want your spouse to know how you feel and what you enjoy, you have to tell him or her. Leave mind reading to the soothsayers.[8]

Sexual compatibility is also formed as couples are sensitive to each other, listen to each other, and try to fulfill each other's sexual desires. It's important to note here that sex is designed to be pleasurable, and couples should attempt to compromise and make sacrifices for each other, but only if it's comfortable for them to do so. This practice will be different and unique to each couple, just as sexual needs and desires are not the same for each person. Nonetheless, increasing sexual compatibility does require work, and it is important to put

---

8   Michele Weiner Davis, *The Sex-Starved Marriage: Boosting Your Marriage Libido* (2004), 185–186.

effort into pleasing each other, trying new things, and attempting to satisfy each other's wants and desires.

Additionally, giving and receiving feedback about your physical relationship is imperative. Discuss what feels good, what you like the most, and what you would like to try, along with what is uncomfortable or not a preference for you. It is important to be sensitive when sharing this information just as it is important to be receptive to feedback from your partner. Responding positively without judgment as your partner makes a request can help ensure emotional safety in talking about such personal thoughts and feelings when it comes to sex.

Finally, increasing emotional intimacy and connection outside the bedroom helps increase physical intimacy inside the bedroom. A marriage must be built on love, mutual respect, sacrifice, trust, and friendship. As you share with and open up to each other about the life you are building together, serve each other, express appreciation and gratitude in your relationship, and provide real acceptance for your partner, you will experience an emotional closeness that will strengthen your physical connection too.

Question #3:
What kinds of affection are appropriate prior to marriage?

PREMARITAL PHYSICAL AFFECTION CAN BE a way to demonstrate love, respect, admiration, and even attraction for each other. Our bodies were created for physical touch to feel good; therefore, it is natural to crave touch and affection. Affection has been defined as "any touch intended to arouse feelings of love in the giver and/or recipient."[1] Therefore, when we refer to physical affection in this chapter, we are not referring to sexual intimacy but instead to nonsexual physical touch between partners. Such affection can be appropriate to express and deepen love and progress a relationship toward marriage. During the engagement process, you are undoubtedly creating a culture of physical touch and defining the role affection will play in your relationship.

Affection has many benefits for the individual as well as the couple. Physical touch has been found to increase a person's positive mood as well as help couples to bond.[2] More specifically, physical touch releases the hormone oxytocin, which then reduces stress and causes a calming sensation. Additionally, affection lowers a person's blood pressure and heart rate.[3] Couples have reported feeling

---

1 Andrew K. Gulledge, Michelle H. Gulledge, & Robert F. Stahmannn, "Romantic Physical Affection Types and Relationship Satisfaction," *The American Journal of Family Therapy*, 31, no. 4 (2003): 233–242, https://www.tandfonline.com/doi/epdf/10.1080/01926180390201936?needAccess=true.
2 *See* M. H. Burleson, W. R. Trevathan, & M. Todd, "In the Mood for Love or Vice Versa? Exploring the Relations Among Sexual Activity, Physical Affection, Affect, and Stress in the Daily Lives of Mid-Aged Women," *Archives of Sexual Behavior*, 36 (2007): 357–368, https://doi.org/10.1007/s10508-006-9071-1.
3 *See* K. C. Light, K. M. Grewen, & J. A. Amico, "More frequent partner hugs and higher oxytocin levels are linked to lower blood pressure and heart rate in premenopausal women," *Biological Psychology*, 69, no. 1 (April 2005): 5–21; https://doi.org/10.1016/j.biopsycho.2004.11.002.

more loved and understood through showing affection toward one another. In fact, research shows that couples who regularly show physical affection have happier and more satisfying relationships.[4]

Principle

Prophet George Albert Smith taught, "Righteousness is the pathway of happiness."[5] Indeed, keeping the commandments brings peace and happiness into our lives. King Benjamin taught, "I would desire that ye should consider on the blessed and happy state of those that keep the commandments of God. For behold, they are blessed in all things, both temporal and spiritual; and if they hold out faithful . . . they are received into heaven, that thereby they may dwell with God in a state of never-ending happiness."[6]

Heavenly Father gives us commandments because He loves us and cares about us, and we strive to keep the commandments to show our love for our Heavenly Father and our faith in Him. One commandment to focus on during the engagement period is the law of chastity, which includes the concept of "complete sexual abstinence before marriage and total fidelity within marriage."[7] Through our actions of maintaining physical boundaries before marriage, we become more of the person God wants us to become.

The root of the law of chastity is self-mastery and self-discipline. President Brigham Young taught, "The [body] must be brought in subjection to the spirit perfectly, or your bodies cannot be raised to inherit eternal life. . . . Seek diligently, until you bring all into subjection to the law of Christ."[8] In the Book of Proverbs, we read, "He that hath no rule over his own spirit is like a city that is broken down, and without walls."[9] We are taught in the New Testament to deny ourselves and take up our crosses[10] and to be temperate.[11] Premarital couples are provided an opportunity of learning to control their sexual desires as they prepare for marriage. As Latter-day Saints, one of our prime duties is to learn to control our appetites, desires, and passions. Each of us must win the battle of the spiritual over the physical. The natural man

---

4 *See* Gullege et al., 2003.
5 George Albert Smith, *Church News*, June 17, 1944, 9.
6 Mosiah 2:41.
7 David A. Bednar, "We Believe in Being Chaste," *Ensign* or *Liahona,* May 2013, 42.
8 Brigham Young, *Teachings of Presidents of the Church: Brigham Young* (1997), 204.
9 Proverbs 25:28.
10 *See* Matthew 16:24.
11 *See* 1 Corinthians 9:25.

within us would have us take the path of least resistance—to be lazy, carnal, and selfish.[12] Conquering our carnal selves requires self-mastery and discipline.

Explanation

Chastity involves loving another person more than we love ourselves, and self-control and self-restraint are crucial to engage in such a deep form of love. Some mistakenly assume that marriage is an unrestrained sexual paradise where anything goes. Marriage and sexual relationships will require self-discipline and restraint throughout a lifespan. To love another person deeply is to put our own needs in their proper place. Elder Richard G. Scott explained, "Let us define love: To love another righteously is to protect, to elevate, to keep pure and undefiled, and to sacrifice one's self for the benefit of the other. To love is to hold in reserve sacred, intimate experiences for the sanctity of marriage."[13]

By keeping the law of chastity during the dating and engagement periods, couples exhibit respect, they signal to each other that they will be true and faithful, and perhaps most importantly, they build trust in each other. President David O. McKay often quoted George Macdonald, who said, "To be trusted is a greater compliment than to be loved."[14] One of the most crucial parts of your relationship will be developing this sacred trust that you will bring into your marriage. Helping each other choose to live the law of chastity is a significant way to begin the formation of that trust.

Sexual relationships prior to marriage can cause physical, emotional, mental, and spiritual challenges. Even if you know that you are getting married, premarital sex can do more damage to your relationship than good. It can jeopardize respect and trust as well as escalate feelings of guilt and shame in the relationship. There also lies a higher risk for breaking up, separation, and increased doubts in your partner by crossing the boundaries couples have set in place. Former Brigham Young University professor Dr. Brent Barlow taught, "Sex is not something we avoid because it is evil. Sex is something we wait for because it is good."[15] Sexual intimacy is something so incredibly beautiful and sacred that our Father in Heaven has reserved it solely for a "man and woman, lawfully wedded as husband and wife."[16] Couples would do well to follow Dr.

---

12 *See* Mosiah 3:19.
13 Richard G. Scott, "To Have Peace and Happiness" (CES Fireside for Young Adults at Brigham Young University, Sept. 12, 2010), 6.
14 David O. McKay, "Character," *True to the Faith* (1966), 274; as cited in Robert E. Wells, "The C's of Spirituality," *Ensign*, Oct. 1978.
15 Brent A. Barlow, *Worth Waiting For* (1995), 75.
16 "The Family: A Proclamation to the World," ChurchofJesusChrist.org.

Barlow's counsel and do all in their power to keep the law of chastity—not because sex is a bad thing, but because it is such a wonderful part of married life.

Practical Application

When it comes to defining what behaviors are appropriate before marriage, and which are not, we should remember the principle taught in the Doctrine and Covenants that states we should *not* be commanded in all things and that we should be "anxiously engaged" in good causes.[17] We are instructed to keep the law of chastity; however, we are not commanded regarding physical affection. Yet if you focus on engaging in positive and appropriate affection before marriage, communicate with your partner about establishing healthy physical boundaries in your relationship, and as a couple, seek to be guided by the Spirit, you will feel more confident in defining what is appropriate and what is not.

Still, in addressing what types of physical affection are appropriate for couples before marriage, let us first explore what is *not* appropriate. To be clear, the principles and doctrines taught in *For the Strength of Youth* apply to every member of the Church—not merely to adolescents!

The new *For the Strength of Youth* defines inappropriate sexual behavior this way: "Outside of marriage between a man and a woman, it is wrong to touch the private, sacred parts of another person's body even if clothed. . . . Avoid anything that purposely arouses lustful emotions in others or yourself."[18]

For the Strength of Youth further advises couples to avoid situations that invite increased temptation. The booklet states, "If you find that situations or activities make temptations stronger, avoid them. You know what those situations and activities are. And if you aren't sure, the Spirit, your parents, and your leaders can help you know."[19]

If couples have crossed the boundary and have committed sexual transgression, know that you can be forgiven! Great hope, happiness, love, and peace come from our Savior, Jesus Christ. We love the wonderful promise from the Book of Isaiah: "Come now, let us reason together, saith the Lord: though your sins be as scarlet, they shall be as white as snow; though they be red like crimson, they shall be as wool."[20]

Premarital couples would do well if they *do not* make physical affection their go-to when they are spending time together. The more time couples

---

17 Doctrine and Covenants 58:26–27.
18 *For the Strength of Youth*, 25.
19 *For the Strength of Youth*, 25.
20 Isaiah 1:18.

spend in physical affection, the less time they are devoting to learning how to communicate with each other. Moreover, most often, couples who spend too much time prior to marriage demonstrating physical affection seem to spend less time solving problems together, planning for the future, being creative, laughing together, participating in fun, meaningful activities, developing their ability to work as a team, setting goals as a couple, serving others, deepening their testimonies, having gospel discussions, and learning to resolve conflict. In fact, when premarital couples spend too much time being physically affectionate, the most important skills to build a future marriage upon become underdeveloped.

Years ago, Dr. Lowell Bennion counseled, "Affection should grow out of genuine friendship and brotherly love, not precede them, if one wishes to be sure of having real and lasting love in marriage."[21] Therefore, the physical affection you show toward each other should not define the relationship, but it should be the natural result of a healthy connection. We are somewhat reticent to give specific directives on what aspects of affection are appropriate because every relationship is so different. However, because the question driving this chapter is what types of premarital affection are appropriate, we feel it is prudent to provide you with some suggestions.

In a research study conducted at Brigham Young University, seven types of physical affection (or nonsexual physical touch) were identified as part of a couple's romantic relationship. These types of physical affection were found to be highly correlated with relationship and partner satisfaction.[22] The seven types of affection included:

1. Back rubs/massages (including back scratches, rubbing your partner's feet, etc.)
2. Caressing (a gentle or loving touch)
3. Cuddling/holding
4. Holding hands
5. Hugging
6. Kissing on lips
7. Kissing on face

This is a great place to start a conversation with your partner about the various types of physical affection identified here. Discuss what types of affection feel loving and positive, and talk to each other about the boundaries you would like to set. You may want to wait to engage in some forms of physical affection

---

21   Lowell Bennion, Q&A: "How much kissing is too much?" *New Era*, Feb. 1971, 5.
22   *See* Gullege et al., 2003.

until after marriage, while expressing a desire to increase other types of affection in your relationship currently. The key is to listen to your partner and respect his or her boundaries in order to reach your potential and, ultimately, the temple. During the engagement process, you should aim to keep a balance between physical affection and all other activities that you engage in. If you can do that, your marriage in the temple can become one of the most spiritually significant days of your entire life.

Question #4:
What should couples talk about before marriage, especially regarding physical intimacy?

Good communication is essential to every healthy relationship. It consists of an exchange of information, thoughts, and feelings between partners. Effective communication helps couples build stronger partnerships and makes it easier to navigate conflict. Edwin O. Haroldsen and Barry L. Johnson, both former professors at Brigham Young University, conducted a survey and found that communication influenced couples' happiness more than any other aspect of marriages they studied. Researchers found that couples who were satisfied with their communication reported feeling happier in their marriages.

In addition, couples who reported strong communication skills also scored high in several other aspects of marriage that were strongly related to happiness. Other marital aspects that were studied included satisfaction with the spouse's personality, the spouse's religious beliefs, the way the married couple resolved conflicts, the management of money, physical intimacy, how the couple spent recreation time, and relationships to children, family, and friends, as well as marital cohesion or closeness.[1] Thus, couples who feel competent in communicating with one another are happier in many other facets of their relationships too.

For every couple, physical intimacy plays a significant role in marriage. Therefore, it is important to address the topic of sex prior to your wedding, even for those couples who are choosing to wait to have sex until they are married. But what, specifically, should these couples discuss when it comes to sex? Some couples may not feel comfortable discussing sexual ideas; after all, they may not have ever talked about such things before. Some may feel that discussing sexual

---

1   *See* Edwin O. Haroldson & Barry L. Johnson, "Talk about Happiness!" *Ensign*, Feb. 1993.

things could lead to a stronger desire to have sex, so they avoid it altogether. Still others, having never been intimate before, may not even know what to say on the subject.

In some ways, sexual discussions prior to marriage could be like going on a vacation to Hawaii—a place you may have never visited. You have heard about the beautiful beaches, and you have read about some of the amazing waterfalls—but you have *never actually been there*. Physical intimacy can work the same way. Most premarital Latter-day Saints have heard about sexual relationships for a long time—but they might have never experienced it, especially not with each other. Therefore, they may not know what to expect or how to communicate about the topic.

Nevertheless, engaging in conversations regarding sexual expectations, attitudes, and beliefs would be valuable prior to marriage. Subjects such as plans and expectations for the honeymoon, expectations of sexual frequency once you are married, birth control, pornography issues, and menstrual cycles are all reasonable topics for discussion. By having such discussions, you are strengthening your communication skills and opening a conversation that you will want to have throughout your lives about your sexual relationship.

Principle

Strong marriages are built on open and honest communication. Such communication can create a foundation of trust and friendship that is crucial for strong and healthy marriages. Many years ago, Elder Marvin J. Ashton, of the Quorum of the Twelve Apostles, explained, "If we would know true love and understanding one for another, we must realize that communication is more than a sharing of words. It is the *wise* sharing of emotions, feelings, and concerns. It is the sharing of oneself totally."[2] True emotional intimacy is sharing your innermost thoughts and feelings with each other on any topic.

In fact, emotional accessibility is more important than sexual accessibility in romantic relationships, and couples are more likely to break up if they struggle to connect emotionally rather than physically. Emotional connection strengthens as communication deepens. It is imperative to be open, be vulnerable, and create a safe space to communicate. Emotional intimacy builds with time as you perceive that your partner truly knows you, understands you, and accepts you for who you are.

---

2 Marvin J. Ashton, *Ensign*, May 1976, 52.

Explanation

Talking about physical intimacy is important before marriage; however, it is not the only topic that should be discussed. We suggest conversing about other subjects too, such as religion, politics, money, family of origin, entertainment, work, education, physical health, raising children, family rituals, and family culture. If premarital couples are over-focused on talking and thinking about their future sexual relationship, they may find it more difficult to keep the boundaries they've set in place regarding their physical relationship. After all, our behaviors are most often driven by what we most often think about and discuss.

Discussions about sex should be appropriate and approached with discernment, common sense, and thoughtfulness. For example, prior to marriage, we recommend that you discuss what your sexual expectations are but avoid getting overly detailed about sexual acts. If a couple has not had sex before, they should talk about what they would like to try but also leave room for adjusting and changing their minds. If one or both partners have had sex before, they may share what was enjoyable and what changes they might prefer in this new intimate relationship. Make sure your partner feels comfortable sharing past sexual experiences with you, without judgment or shame. Again, sexual details are not important, but sharing one's sexual thoughts and desires are crucial to the conversation. In addition, once you are married and sexually active, sexual dialogues will naturally become more specific, and you will have a better idea of what you should be discussing. It is important to note here that couples should avoid engaging in phone-sex conversations or sexting. Detail-oriented descriptions of what will happen in the bedroom set premarital couples up for increased arousal, difficulty keeping boundaries, and possible disappointment later.

More importantly, discuss what you know about sex, how your family talked about sex growing up, and if you have any questions or concerns about physical intimacy. Talking about sex prior to marriage will help you to continue that conversation about sex after you are married. We simply suggest that you keep a proper balance in what you do discuss. If you are having a conversation about sex prior to marriage, make sure you follow up that conversation with discussing other topics too. There is much, much more to marriage than sex—although that is an important part of it. Communication in all areas of your relationship will help improve your communication about physical intimacy too. Once married, conversations about this sacred topic can bring you even closer together and create a strong bond of intimacy.

Practical Application

To improve communication skills before marriage, we have listed ten general topics with questions for you to consider discussing with your partner, including sex. It is important to note that there are no right or wrong answers, nor are your answers a binding contract at this time. Partners may change their views throughout the marriage; therefore, it is important to continue addressing these topics even after the wedding.

1. Religion:
    - Do you have a current temple recommend, and how important is it to you to keep it current? How often do you attend the temple, and what are your plans for us to attend the temple together?
    - How do you choose to live the Word of Wisdom?
    - How do you choose when to wear your garments and when not to?
    - Do you tithe on gross or net income, and when do you choose to pay it?
    - How do you define keeping the Sabbath day holy in your life?
    - How important are the daily habits of scripture study and prayer to you?
    - How do you observe fast Sunday?
    - How do you want to implement family home evening, *Come, Follow Me* lessons, and ministering?
    - What role do the Church leaders play in your life? Is there anything you currently disagree with regarding Church leaders?
    - Do you believe in always accepting callings? What callings would be hard for you to accept? If I were called into leadership (for example, in Relief Society, Young Women, Young Men, Primary, elders quorum, bishopric), would you be willing to sustain and support me in my calling?
    - How do you feel about priesthood blessings, and when is it appropriate to ask for one? Whom do you feel comfortable asking for a priesthood blessing?
2. Politics:
    - How passionate are you about politics? Do your political beliefs align with a particular political party?
    - How do you feel about the importance of voting? Whom have you voted for in past presidential or local elections?
    - What are your views on abortion, immigration, gun control, healthcare, climate change, etc.?

- Where do you get your political ideology, and what are the political views of your family of origin?
- How would you feel if we voted differently from each other?
- Do you feel your political beliefs line up well with the gospel of Jesus Christ?

3. Money:
    - How much debt do you have?
    - Have you ever declared bankruptcy, and if so, what was the reason?
    - What kind of debt are you comfortable with having?
    - How much money do you put into savings, or how much money have you currently saved?
    - What are your feelings about keeping a budget?
    - What are your plans regarding saving for our retirement?
    - How much money did your parents make growing up, and how much do you expect us to make as a couple?
    - What do you define as a comfortable lifestyle regarding money?
    - What kind of lifestyle do you hope we will live one day?
    - What do you hope we will be able to do with our money to make a difference in the world?

4. Family of Origin:
    - What practices and traditions from your family do you hope to bring into our marriage?
    - Are there practices and traditions from your family that you hope we do not incorporate?
    - Did you have family dinner growing up, and how do you want to implement family dinners for our family?
    - What was your family's beliefs about work and chores?
    - What was your family's belief about recreation and fun?
    - What kind of pets did you have as a child? Do you want pets, and if so, what kind?
    - What roles do you see your parents and my parents playing in our marriage and family?
    - How will we handle conflict within our family of origin?
    - What are your feelings regarding living close or farther away from our families? How much time do you see us spending with each other's families?
    - Is there anything in your past you think I should know?

5. Entertainment:
    - How would you define appropriate entertainment?
    - Do you watch rated-R movies or mature (MA) television shows, and what exceptions do you make, if any at all?
    - What type of music do you listen to, and how do you feel about other types of music?
    - What are your boundaries around appropriate media, such as movies, television, music, and social media?
    - How do you feel about having televisions in our home, and where would it be appropriate to have them in the house? How do you feel about having a television in our bedroom?
    - How do you feel about video games?
    - What boundaries do you have around electronic use for yourself, and what would you think would be appropriate for our children regarding electronic time?
    - How do you feel about the use of social media and cell phones in our relationship? Are there any boundaries you feel we should establish?
6. Work and Education:
    - How important is getting an education to you?
    - Are you willing to work to support our family if the need arises?
    - What are your five-, ten-, and fifteen-year plans for education and career?
    - How can we achieve a work-life balance for our family?
    - What roles do you see yourself fulfilling in the home? What roles do you see me fulfilling in the home?
    - What are your expectations if one of us stays at home with the children?
    - How will chores be divided? Are there certain chores that you do not want to do?
7. Physical Health:
    - How do you feel about going to see a doctor when you are sick?
    - Do you have any medical or psychological diagnoses that you have not shared with me yet?
    - What are your views on vaccines?
    - Are your views of medicine more Western (doctors, hospitals, and medication) or Eastern (meditation, lifestyle, and naturalistic)?

- How do you feel about your body? What do you like about it or not like about it? Have you ever experienced an eating disorder?
- How important is my body image to you?
- How do you plan to incorporate exercise in your life, and how do you plan to stay healthy? Would you like to belong to a health club? What is your go-to form of exercise?
- What are your thoughts on diets and our family eating habits?
- How will you act if I gain weight? What are your expectations surrounding my weight, if any?
- How do you feel about relaxation? How do you see us relaxing as a couple?

8. Children:
    - When would you like to start having children? How many children do you want?
    - How do you foresee us teaching our children the gospel and establishing a gospel-centered home?
    - Do you have any traditions of naming children in your family, and would you like to continue those traditions?
    - Were you spanked as a child, and do you think it is an appropriate form of discipline?
    - How do you feel about our children playing sports? Which ones would you like them to participate in?
    - What role do you want music to play in our children's lives? Will we have them learn how to play specific instruments?
    - What are your views on schooling our kids—home, public, or private?
    - How do you feel about swearing and about our children swearing?
    - How would you feel or respond if one or more of our children is gay or transgender?
    - How would you feel or respond if one or more of our children chose not to continue being a member of our Church?

9. Family Rituals and Culture:
    - How does your family celebrate birthdays? How would you like us to celebrate birthdays in our family?
    - How does your family celebrate Mother's Day and Father's Day? Do they buy gifts? How do you see us celebrating Mother's Day and Father's Day?

- How do your parents celebrate their anniversary? How would you like us to celebrate our anniversary each year?
- What are your holiday traditions? How do you want to celebrate each holiday in our family?
- Do you want to visit your family for any holidays? If so, which ones?
- Which holiday is most important to you, and why?
- How does your family observe baby blessings and baptisms? Would you like to continue those traditions?
- How important are vacations to you? How much should they cost? How often do you want to go? Do you prefer traveling locally, stateside, or internationally? What do you like to do on vacations—relax, sightsee, or both?
- What do you consider grounds for divorce? How would you define cheating and infidelity?
- How do you feel about meeting with a therapist if I think it would be helpful?

10. Sex:
    - How do you feel about our boundaries as we strive to keep the law of chastity?
    - How did you learn about sex? What do you know about sex?
    - Did your family talk about sex, and if so, how did they talk about it growing up?
    - From a future husband: What is your menstrual cycle like, and how does it affect you? Is there anything I need to know about this part of your life?
    - What should I know about your dating history and sexual past? Have you had sexual intercourse with anyone?
    - Has pornography ever been a part of your life? What about masturbation? Do you feel you have ever been addicted to these practices? Have you received the proper help to overcome these problems?
    - What are your thoughts about birth control? What types of birth control do you feel comfortable using?
    - What do you expect to happen sexually on our wedding night and honeymoon? What do you expect from me on our honeymoon?
    - What do you think our sexual life will be like once we are married? What are you expecting from each of us? What are you looking forward to or anticipating?

- Do you have any concerns about being intimate, and if so, what are they?
- How will we handle disagreements and concerns with our intimate life?
- How do you feel that stress, children, and other pressures will affect the frequency and quality of our sexual lives?

These questions, as well as others, can be most helpful in exploring your feelings and attitudes about a myriad of subjects. It is not crucial that you agree on every topic. What is most important is that you can discuss these topics objectively and empathetically. As you talk about these issues, you can draw closer together, learn to understand each other, and begin to build a wonderful, Christ-centered marriage and family together.

Question #5:
What if you are fairly naïve and don't know what to do the first time you have sex?

MARK AND HIS WIFE, JANIE, had the following experience with one of their daughters. It was the night before their daughter's wedding, and Mark and Janie were having a "sex" discussion with her prior to her wedding day. The more they talked, the more Mark and Janie were amazed at how little their daughter seemed to know about sexual things. After all, over the years, they had several discussions with their daughter about sexual intimacy. As parents, they were a bit bewildered that their daughter was quite naïve. After their discussion was over, Mark and Janie hugged their daughter, and she left the room. These parents looked at each other, shrugged their shoulders, and then Janie said, "Oh my goodness; I hope she's going to be okay." Mark responded, "I'm sure they will figure out their sexual relationship, but it may take some time." That experience occurred over five years ago. That daughter and her husband now have four children. Lesson: no matter how naïve individuals may be about the sexual relationship, people tend to figure things out!

We have learned from some of our students that one of their main concerns as they approach physical intimacy is that they simply do not know how to have sex. They are worried that they do not understand some of the basics of human intimacy as they enter into a sexual relationship. Some are embarrassed by their lack of knowledge, while others are on the verge of panic. Still others laugh it off and assume that everything will probably work out, while others avoid the topic altogether. Even though these reactions to the unknown may be common, what an individual may not know can be learned.

Principle
"The glory of God is intelligence."[1] Becoming educated about this sacred topic can help alleviate concerns; by gaining knowledge about intimacy, we

---
1 Doctrine and Covenants 93:36.

can increase our intelligence. Elder David A. Bednar has said, "Intelligence also means applying the knowledge we obtain for righteous purposes."[2] Learning about physical intimacy and applying that knowledge to your marital relationship is indeed a righteous purpose to help you bond together as husband and wife. Our Heavenly Father wants us to gain knowledge and experience in this life; that knowledge is portable. What we learn in this life will remain with us for eternity. And yes, that includes knowledge about intimacy.

We live in a world that revels in sexuality and ridicules morality. Sexual content permeates television, music, movies, and social media. Unfortunately, most of this "prime time" sexual content is tainted by worldly, wicked, and carnal perspectives. In short, it is neither wholesome nor real. In our day, there are few voices that provide a divine or even wholesome perspective regarding sexuality. Such viewpoints, as well as a lack of useful information, can contribute to the worries and concerns that many couples carry into the honeymoon and their sexual lives thereafter.

You are now entering a dimension of marriage that will require knowledge, wisdom, and even skills. Yes, to understand human intimacy and prepare for it, you will have to learn some new things. In fact, as you approach marriage, learning about the sexual relationship will most likely influence your marital happiness and satisfaction. The fact that you are reading this book demonstrates that you are willing to learn, gain knowledge, and improve!

Explanation

Latter-day Saints view marital intimacy as a sacred union that is to be shared only within the bounds of marriage. Once you are married, you have the right and privilege to share physical, spiritual, mental, and emotional expressions with the love of your life—your eternal companion. In a marriage relationship, it is appropriate, and even encouraged, to discuss sexual intimacy openly with your spouse, as this will be the best and most effective learning tool you can have. Busby, Carroll, and Leavitt have explained,

> Sexually mature spouses express love in ways that build the relationship and add to the foundation of positive sexual symbolism. Such expressions of love are measured by the *quality of the communication* between spouses and their ability *to manage differences and conflict.* . . . Sexual wholeness requires kind and

---

[2] David A. Bednar, "The Glory of God is Intelligence," *Liahona*, Oct. 2007.

candid communication about the sexual relationship—both during as well as in between sexual encounters.[3]

Our Father in Heaven has instilled into your soul, your constitution, your anatomy, the desire to express physical love in a very profound way. Most likely, your future spouse will have similar concerns regarding intimacy. Like you, they, too, may not know much about the sexual relationship—that is what can make this adventure exciting. Both husband and wife must accept the role of being a good teacher and a willing student in the realm of sexual intimacy. You will learn things about each other that no one else can possibly know and, in some cases, cannot be found in a book. As you learn from each other, intimacy can become a wonderful and fulfilling experience for both husband and wife. No one else can really explain to you in detail what emotions and feelings will be generated within you or your new spouse, or how your body will respond to new stimuli, or how these expressions will greatly enrich your marriage.

First, we should emphasize that most of the learning about the sexual relationship will transpire after you are married. It isn't necessary to know everything about sex prior to marriage. In fact, too much preoccupation about sex prior to marriage could lead to breaking the law of chastity. So, be patient! This newfound knowledge will come soon enough. Once you're married and you can engage sexually together, you will come to understand how your bodies will respond to these sexual and romantic expressions of love. Intimacy is certainly a learn-as-you-go experience, and the more educated you become, the more confidence you will gain. And your worries and concerns will subside. Much of the excitement about the sexual relationship is that you will be able to learn about this new part of your relationship together.

Practical Application

The more you learn about the sacred subject of physical intimacy, the more knowledge and confidence you will acquire. Here are a few basic principles that could help alleviate your worries and concerns as you prepare for sexual intimacy:

1. *Read a good book on marital intimacy.* We have provided a list of good books in chapter seven of this work. Reading and learning about sex will help provide you with a strong intellectual understanding of physical intimacy and will lay a foundation that you can build

---

3   D. M. Busby, J. S. Carroll, & C. Leavitt, *Sexual Wholeness in Marriage: An LDS Perspective on Integrating Sexuality and Spirituality in our Marriages* (2013), 121.

upon throughout your marriage. You may want to read these books separately before marriage and together after marriage. Nevertheless, it is important to discuss what you have learned or address any questions you may have with your partner. We recommend that after marriage you continue to read and learn about this sacred area of marriage.

2. *Prepare personally for the unknown.* If you feel like you do not know what to do when it comes to sex, you are not alone. It is common to feel this way when you are embarking on a new journey. It would be helpful to reflect on other times in your life that you faced the unknown and did not know what to expect. How did you prepare? What did it feel like, and how did you navigate your way through it? How were you able to relax and enjoy the experience, or how did you adapt and make changes? Gathering personal experiences where you have encountered unfamiliar situations and navigated your way through them successfully will help build your confidence when it comes to approaching the unfamiliar territory of physical intimacy. Even more, share some of these experiences with your partner and explore how your partner approaches new situations as well.

3. *Gather information from parents* (or someone you admire, trust, and respect). Some parents can be gun-shy when it comes to helping their children prepare for their honeymoon and initial intimate encounters. Most likely, this is not because of their lack of knowledge; after all, they have been through the experience themselves. Instead, their reticence could stem from their concern over what to say, when to say it, or their fear of sharing too much. Some parents may not feel confident that they can explain or teach about sexual relationships adequately. Other parents could be wonderfully open, honest, and direct about the sexual experience. It is helpful to have someone you trust respond to your basic questions and assist you in developing a healthy attitude as you approach physical intimacy. Even after you are married, it could still be helpful to discuss the topic of physical intimacy with your parents or someone you trust, as you may have additional questions or uncertainties. Discussing such matters with parents can become a bonding and edifying experience.

4. *Communication with your spouse is one of the greatest keys to sexual fulfillment.* If couples want to meet each other's sexual desires, they will need to communicate with each other. Sexual expectations and concerns certainly need to be discussed; these conversations can

alleviate anxiety and help both partners feel comfortable and confident. Although these conversations may be awkward at first, this kind of dialogue is the essence of deep emotional connection and intimacy. Doug and Dr. Stephen Lamb wrote,

> The importance of talking together, sharing information, and instructing each other cannot be overemphasized. Each spouse should openly share his or her needs and wants, not only in the first few days of marriage, but throughout their life together. Each partner should regularly inquire, in a sensitive way, how the spouse feels and what can be done to help the companion find greater joy and fulfillment in the sexual experience.[4]

Although you may read books and talk to friends or family members, physical intimacy will be a new and unique experience for both of you—even if one or both of you was married before. Learning about the key principles of the sexual relationship and discussing them with each other will increase your knowledge and clarify your expectations. Such discussions will prepare each of you for your honeymoon, as well as for a lifelong sexual relationship. Once married, you will want to have further discussions regarding what is stimulating and pleasurable or irritating and uncomfortable—for both of you. Because this is new territory, a spirit of humility, forgiveness, patience, and a sincere desire to learn from each other can help to make this a special bonding experience for both husband and wife.

---

4   Stephen E. Lamb & Douglas E. Brinley, *Between Husband and Wife: Gospel Perspectives on Marital Intimacy* (2000), 46.

Question #6:
What if you feel anxious or scared about having sex?

HUMAN BEINGS ARE ALWAYS A little unnerved in beginning a new adventure where they have little or no experience. For example, most people have worries and concerns when they begin a new school year, start a new job, accept a Church calling, or enter a new relationship. Beginning an intimate, sexual relationship with your future spouse is no different. It is completely normal to have some apprehension, anxiety, and fear about being married and entering into a sexual relationship with a partner. Many individuals fear the unknown, and sexual intimacy is an unknown area to many Latter-day Saints. If one or both partners have had past sexual experiences, anxious feelings still may exist regarding sex with a brand-new partner. Nevertheless, these intimate concerns can be alleviated through preparation, information, and communication.

Principle

Remember, "if ye are prepared ye shall not fear."[1] A sexual relationship requires extreme vulnerability, where couples share their physical, emotional, spiritual, and mental selves. Nevertheless, Doctrine and Covenants 38:30 reminds us that if we are prepared, we have no need for fear or worry. In 2 Timothy 1:7, we read that, "God hath not given us the spirit of fear; but of power, and of love, and of a sound mind." Our Father in Heaven does not want us to be fearful about anything. Instead, He wants us to move forward with faith and confidence. When husbands and wives engage in sexual intimacy, they should be assured that this connection is God-ordained and God-blessed.

Anxiety regarding intimacy often comes from unfortunate rumors, possibly exaggerated and negative stories we have heard from others, and perhaps from media sources. Our fears and anxieties can also be based in our lack of

---

1 Doctrine and Covenants 38:30.

understanding of the sexual relationship, from lack of knowledge and information, and perhaps from many other unknowns. This is not to say people do not have sexual experiences that are unfulfilling or unsatisfying. In fact, it is possible this happens to all couples; however, the key is how both partners communicate about it, learn from it, and make adjustments so they can have the best sexual experiences together.

Explanation

When we fall in love, there arises in us a physical desire, as well as emotional and spiritual impressions, to be a married couple, to engage in the most intimate of physical acts, and to create a family of our own. How can we be a husband or wife and not share everything, even our bodies and souls, with each other? Isn't that what "becoming one" is all about? We may understand these principles in theory; however, once married, we now move past theory to actual application and implementation. Such enactment can be intimidating. Just ask anyone standing in their wedding reception line early in the evening, knowing that, before the night is over, perhaps the couple will have done things that were beyond their comprehension a short time ago.

Sharing ourselves in an intimate way with a spouse can bring forth natural concerns, such as feelings of inadequacy, disappointing our partner, perhaps body-image issues, whether we or our new spouse will know what to do, how we will treat each other, and how we will respond to this sacred and special experience. Additionally, we may be concerned about what expectations we both have regarding frequency, sexual-arousal techniques, and a host of other aspects that will surface. This is particularly true where both parties have never had a sexual relationship. Some, perhaps, have even had negative experiences with previous sexual partners or, even more challenging, some have experienced past sexual trauma.

Another difficulty could come from our Latter-day Saint culture or our religious beliefs. For example, some may feel that the sexual relationship is wicked, perverse, or sinful. Perhaps Church leaders, teachers, or family members who have had negative sexual experiences have conveyed adverse sexual messages. Such negative sexual conditioning leads to negative thoughts and feelings about sex and our bodies, often resulting in an inhibited sexual response in marriage.[2]

Practical Application

One of the most important ways to alleviate fears and concerns about your honeymoon and the following sexual experiences will be to discuss them

---

2   *See* Laura M. Brotherson, *And They Were Not Ashamed: Strengthening Marriage through Sexual Fulfillment* (2004), 2.

with each other. Perhaps these worries could be written down on paper and then talked about. Remember to focus on "I feel" statements, where you share your feelings with your partner. It may look like this:

- I am scared sex will be painful.
- I feel inadequate because I don't know how to please you physically.
- I am worried I will do something you don't like.
- I feel insecure about you seeing me completely naked.
- I am afraid I won't be able to orgasm and that will make you feel bad.
- I feel uncertain I will live up to your expectations sexually.
- I feel overwhelmed with everything I need to learn sexually so I can be a good partner in bed.

Discuss these kinds of feelings, listen to each other, and provide that reassurance your partner needs to feel connected to you. This will ensure that when or if any of these worries become a reality, you can be there for each other emotionally and not just physically.

One of our own children had concerns prior to her wedding. As she expressed these concerns to her fiancé, he said, in a very soft and comforting way, "Do you trust me?" She said, "Yes, I do." Then he promised her that they would figure out the sexual part of their lives together and that he would never do anything to violate her trust or make her feel uncomfortable. Thus, it is important to address each other's worries or concerns and establish a safe space to talk about them.

Others in your life could be of assistance as well. You could convey your concerns with loving and understanding parents or siblings, other married family members or friends you trust, Church leaders you can confide in, or even a professional counselor. They can help lessen fears and worries and provide reassurance about how this aspect of marriage can bless the relationship, not only during the honeymoon phase, but also in the years that follow.

Mark and his wife, Janie, shared the following experience:

> When our oldest daughter was about to get married, Janie and I had a wonderful talk with her the night before her wedding. She confided in us that she was extremely anxious about her upcoming wedding night because of some horror stories she had been told. I asked my daughter who told her these terrible "tales," and she mentioned the names of several girls I recognized as her roommates and friends. I said, "Wait

a minute, Brittany. None of those girls are even married!" My daughter confirmed my suspicion, and we had a good laugh to lighten the moment. Brittany later reported that she and Tyler had a wonderful honeymoon, and she could not believe she had worked herself up so much—she was really afraid!

Remember, there is no reason to fear if you are prepared. Preparation should include a physical examination prior to marriage for the bride-to-be, preferably with a gynecologist, who is a specialist in women's reproductive anatomy. All our bodies have been created a little differently, and there are some women who have a difficult time and possibly experience some pain when they begin to have a sexual relationship. Gynecologists are prepared to answer questions you may have about sex, birth control, and the possibility of pain with sexual intercourse. At times, gynecologists may recommend a series of stretching implements that prepare a woman's body for sex or other medical procedures that would benefit your body in a way that would make the sexual experience more pleasurable.

Furthermore, some people experience negative thoughts or irrational thought patterns, called cognitive distortions, that increase anxiety. Cognitive distortions can also occur regarding our thoughts about sex. It is helpful to address these inaccurate and false beliefs in order to challenge their validity and replace them with rational and realistic thoughts. There are different types of cognitive distortions, but we highlighted eight of them below to show how they can affect sexual anxiety:

1. *All-or-nothing thinking* includes the extreme thoughts of "always" or "never." One might believe they will "never" be able to please their partner, sex "always" has to be amazing, their partner is "never" in the mood for sex, or sex "always" means having an orgasm. These "always" and "never" statements contribute to black-and-white thinking but do not leave much room for gray areas and can affect physical intimacy in a negative way.

2. *Overgeneralizations* consist of making broad interpretations from a single event or from only a few events. For example, "I felt awkward during sex, so I am an awkward person when it comes to physical intimacy." Or, "That sexual experience was somewhat uncomfortable, so sex is uncomfortable for me and my body." Overgeneralizing results in a hopeless feeling that one experience applies to all future experiences.

3. *Disqualifying the positive* recognizes only the negative aspects of a situation while ignoring the positive ones. For example, if your partner compliments something that you did sexually that felt good and then asks for you to do something different as well, you might focus on the thought that your partner is unsatisfied instead of hearing the positive compliments or the positive feedback your partner has shared with you.
4. *Jumping to conclusions* occurs when we interpret the meaning of a situation with little or no evidence. One might jump to conclusions when their partner is not in the mood to have sex to mean their partner is not attracted to them or in love with them like they used to be. Jumping to conclusions is damaging because it involves reading into situations and associating false meanings or interpretations.
5. *Emotional reasoning* occurs when we believe our feelings are facts. A person may feel inadequate when it comes to sex and then reason they are a worthless lover, or someone may feel lonely and then believe their partner does not want to be around them. Our feelings need to be validated, but that does not mean they are factual in what they represent.
6. *Should statements* are beliefs that things should be a certain way. When it comes to sex, believing that our sexual experiences should follow a certain template sets us up for disappointment, shame, and failed expectations. For example, he "should" be romantic, she "should" like this sexual position, I "should" have sex every day, or we "should" both have orgasms at the same time. "Should" statements only lead to frustration and resentment between partners.
7. *Personalization* happens when a person takes everything personally as an indicator of their inadequacy. For example, if a husband has difficulty maintaining an erection, a wife might think she is to blame or that he is not attracted to her. However, there are many circumstances that are not anyone's fault or under anyone's control, and taking them personally only further creates hurt and disconnection.
8. *Labeling* occurs when we judge ourselves or our partner and affix a negative, unreasonable label. For example, "I am a bad lover," "My partner is lazy in bed," or "My partner is selfish because he or she wanted to be pleasured first." Labels reflect a negative perception that

partners have for each other, but those perceptions are harder to change after that labeling has occurred.[3]

Cognitive distortions can lead to negative feelings, thoughts, and behaviors between married partners regarding sex, thereby contributing to feelings of anxiety and directly affecting your sex life. The chemicals released with anxiety reduce sexual desire, affect the ability for arousal and orgasm, and prevent you from staying in the present and connected to your partner. Thus, it is important to be aware of the irrational thoughts and replace them with clearer, more realistic thoughts about sex. Find evidence to prove the negative thought is wrong or unsupported and replace it with a more positive one. For instance, "My partner is not in the mood to have sex right now, but she or he may be later"; "I didn't have an orgasm, but that really felt good"; "That felt awkward or a bit uncomfortable, so next time, we will try something different"; "When my partner expresses a sexual desire, it means he or she trusts me enough to share that information with me, not that he or she is unsatisfied." Positive thinking takes effort, but creating this habit regarding your concerns about physical intimacy will help reduce the anxiety and, thus, reduce the power it has to influence your intimate life.

Your worries and fears are natural, but information, knowledge, and shared experiences will help prepare you and give you confidence to engage in the physically intimate part of your life. Remember when you learned to ride a bicycle? We will assume that you did not just hop on the bike and ride it five miles down the road. Like most of us, you probably fell a few times, accumulated some scrapes and bruises, but got back on the bike and kept trying. Over a short period, you learned to hold the handlebars steadier, and you pedaled farther than the time before. Soon, you did not even notice that you were trying to balance. Months later, riding your bike became second nature. Your sex life will work in a similar fashion. There may be some figurative bumps and bruises along the way, but soon enough, you will figure it out, and it can become a wonderful part of your shared life together.

---

3   David Burns, *The Feeling Good Handbook* (2012).

Question #7:
Now that we are engaged, how can we best prepare for intimacy?

THERE ARE MANY DECISIONS TO make and topics to discuss before couples are married. For instance, when and where will they marry? Where will they live? How will they provide for themselves and stick close to a budget? Education, religious beliefs and practices, household responsibilities, decision-making processes, in-law relationships, birth control, and when to begin their family are all high on the list of matters to discuss. While we certainly hope couples will spend some quality time addressing these important issues, the focus of this book is to help couples prepare for sexual intimacy.

Principle

Preparation is the key to success in any area of life—especially in matters of intimacy. In Doctrine and Covenants 109:8, we read, "Organize yourselves; prepare every needful thing, and establish a house, even a house of prayer, a house of fasting, a house of faith, a house of learning, a house of glory, a house of order, a house of God." This verse can become the blueprint for creating an ideal home, marriage, and family life. We believe that when it comes to "preparing every needful thing" in marriage, a healthy sexual relationship should be an important part of marital preparation.

Being prepared is one of the bedrock principles for Latter-day Saints. Preparation, or even prevention, is one of the greatest interventions for most problems that married couples will experience. Although there are many reasons why people divorce, any amateur Google search will reveal that sexual problems are often mentioned as a cause for marital tension and disharmony. We hope that young couples will understand the impact sexual issues can have on a marriage—for better or for worse.

Furthermore, if there are sexual matters to deal with in a marriage, marriage partners cannot bury their heads in the sand or hope that their problems will just go away. Successful couples can recognize problems in their marriages and have the courage to address them. Therefore, if you understand the impact sexual issues could have on a marriage, decide to be prepared before you are married!

Explanation

There are several ways that married couples can prepare for intimacy—without being intimate. Perhaps the most important is to prepare spiritually through a desire to include the Lord in a couple's relationship. By placing the Savior at the center of their lives, their desire to pray, read the scriptures, and focus on the sacred sealing ordinance in the temple should begin to weigh on their minds and hearts. We believe one of the most significant practices a couple could do to prepare for their celestial marriage is to read and study Doctrine and Covenants 131 and 132. Learn about the sacred ordinance of temple marriage, the covenants made, and the blessings associated with keeping those covenants.

In addition, it is important to recognize that sexuality is God-ordained. Our Father in Heaven not only created us, but He created the sacred, intimate relationship between husband and wife. President Spencer W. Kimball endorsed a healthy sexual relationship between a man and woman when he said, "It is the destiny of men and women to join together to make eternal family units. In the context of lawful marriage, the intimacy of sexual relations is right and divinely approved. There is nothing unholy or degrading about sexuality in itself, for by that means men and women join in a process of creation and in an expression of love."[1] If a healthy sexual relationship is part of our "destiny," as President Kimball mentioned, then it certainly should be something that we prepare for and take seriously.

Preparation includes learning about sex and gaining knowledge about the physical aspect of intimacy, specifically the sexual response cycle, and the anatomy of sex. Becoming sexually educated and informed will enhance your future sexual relationship and increase your comfortability and familiarity with the sexual dynamics of men and women. There are several books that we would like to recommend that provide specific information and insight:

- *Between Husband & Wife: Gospel Perspectives on Marital Intimacy* by Stephen E. Lamb and Douglas E. Brinley

---

1 Spencer W. Kimball, *President Kimball Speaks Out* (1981), 2.

- *The Act of Marriage* by Tim F. and Beverly LaHaye
- *Becoming One: Intimacy in Marriage* by Robert F. Stahmann, Wayne R. Young, and Julie G. Grover
- *Intended for Pleasure* by Ed Wheat and Gaye Wheat
- *And They Were Not Ashamed: Strengthening Marriage Through Sexual Fulfillment* by Laura M. Brotherson

Additionally, we recommend that you identify a person whom you can trust to have frank and open conversations regarding intimacy. This individual could be a parent, a sibling, or a close friend. It is important that the person whom you trust has a healthy view about sexual relationships; otherwise, you may be receiving information that could be discouraging and confusing. Whatever knowledge you can gain from your trusted friend will help you to be more prepared for sex and approach physical intimacy in a healthy way.

Now, a word of caution on this topic. Just because you read a book and talk to an expert or two does not mean you will become a skilled lover with an A+ rating overnight. Like anything else in life, developing a healthy and positive intimate life with your spouse requires time, effort, energy, and much discussion. Doug and Dr. Stephen Lamb have explained,

> Couples shouldn't worry if they don't know everything about sex during their engagement and courtship. Frankly, they don't need to. It's quite normal to still have many questions about what lies ahead right up until the wedding day, and even after that. That's one purpose of the honeymoon: it gives husband and wife a chance to discover the sexual aspect of the relationship together. Sexual intimacy in marriage is a journey, not a destination.[2]

Moreover, be courageous enough to broach the topic of intimacy with your fiancé. Preparation for intimacy prior to marriage takes open communication between both partners. It is important to address with each other your thoughts, feelings, and expectations about the sexual relationship. Due to your gender, culture, upbringing, personal experiences, and perhaps some beliefs that have been passed down to you from others, you both may have different ideas and expectations about the sexual relationship. Addressing the topic of intimacy with your partner can also help you identify any negative attitudes, reservations, or

---

2 S. E. Lamb & D. E. Brinley, *Between Husband and Wife: Gospel Perspectives on Marital Intimacy* (2008), 51.

concerns regarding intimacy that you may have. If these challenges do surface, it might be helpful to talk to someone about them, such as a parent, a friend, or a counselor, and attempt to work through and resolve these issues.

Indeed, the very best preparation for physical intimacy will come once you are married and can navigate this path together. We have seen too many couples who seem to spend more time preparing for sexual intimacy than preparing to be married. Much of their discretionary time is spent talking about what life will be like when they can be intimate. In some cases, these couples are so hyper-focused on sex they have given little thought to budgets, communication, resolving conflict, spirituality, traditions, physical health, or where to live.

Couples who obsess over the sexual relationship prior to their marriage often find out after marriage that they do not have as much in common in their personalities as they initially thought. Some couples learn too soon that their relationship is underdeveloped. Such couples will need to spend time strengthening these other dimensions of their relationship. Remember that it is much better to come into marriage a little naïve as to the mechanics of sex, but to be strong in your communication, problem-solving skills, affection toward each other, and commitment to the gospel of Jesus Christ. Those communication skills will help you overcome a multitude of problems in many dimensions of your marriage.

Practical Application

In summary, the greatest sexual preparation will not occur until after you are married and can have a sexual relationship. However, before that day comes, we would encourage you to do the following:

1. *Prepare Spiritually:*
   - Continue to strengthen your relationship with the Lord through prayer and reading your scriptures. Learn about the sacred ordinance of temple marriage (such as through reading Doctrine and Covenants 131 and 132) and focus on its eternal blessings.
   - Recognize sexuality is God-ordained, and it is meant to be pleasurable and bond husbands and wives together.
2. *Prepare by Gaining Knowledge about Physical Intimacy:*
   - Read books that have been written in a positive light and through the lens of faith about intimacy between husband and wife. You might want to read these books on your own before marriage and then read them together after marriage.

- Have a frank and open conversation about sex with a parent, sibling, or close friend. Keep in mind, everyone's experiences are different. However, being able to have your questions answered will help you know more about what to expect.
3. *Prepare by Communicating:*
    - Talk about your thoughts, feelings, and expectations about the sexual relationship. Discuss how your gender, culture, beliefs, upbringing, and personal experiences contribute to your ideas and expectations about sex. Prior to marriage, it is preferable to have these conversations in an appropriate setting, such as during the day or in a public space where you can maintain privacy yet uphold boundaries regarding your physical relationship.
    - Be willing to talk with a parent, friend, or counselor about your own sexual issues if you have any issues that need to be worked through.
    - Revisit your expectations regarding intimacy after you are married. You should expect that your expectations will change once you are married and during your lifespan. Therefore, couples should discuss their marital and sexual expectations frequently.
4. *Remember That Sexual Preparation Is Only One Part of the More Significant Topic of Marital Preparation.*

Preparing for marital intimacy can be an exciting adventure as you begin your life together. As with learning anything new, there will be adjustments to make and lessons to learn. That is perfectly fine! Almost every married couple has had to navigate the same path and learn some of the same lessons you will learn. A healthy sexual relationship is something every couple should anticipate. A good, healthy, sexual relationship, "within the proper boundaries, will help keep your marriage strong and will improve many aspects of your marriage. It will help you reduce the importance of the other problems you face. It will help bind you together such that you can surmount other life challenges as a team."[3]

---

3   R. F. Stahmann, W. R. Young, & J. G. Grover, *Becoming One: Intimacy in Marriage* (2004), 11.

Question #8:
How should a couple prepare and plan for the honeymoon?

THE HONEYMOON IS A TRADITION among many cultures for the newlywed couple to spend time together alone after the wedding festivities are over. Planning and executing a wedding can be an exciting and special time, but it also can be stressful, exhausting, and overwhelming. The honeymoon is typically a vacation planned for the couple to relax, to bond in a new way, to create their first memories of marriage, and to celebrate their new identity as a married couple. Couples experience many "firsts" during the honeymoon, such as being called, "Mr. and Mrs.," as they check into the hotel for the first time as husband and wife. A bride may begin to introduce herself with her new last name. The couple sleeps in the same bed for the first time and wakes up together the next morning. In addition, the honeymoon is often the first time the couple is vacationing together alone, and it also marks the couple's start of living with one another day in and day out.

The honeymoon is also an opportunity for couples to connect both emotionally and physically. The honeymoon, or even the wedding night before the honeymoon really begins, will, in many cases, be the first occasion for a newlywed couple to be sexually intimate. This is an exciting time in life, filled with anxious anticipation, happiness, joy, and some uncertainty. However, as you plan and prepare for your honeymoon and set realistic expectations, couples will often reflect on their honeymoon as a shared positive experience that brought them closer together.

Principle

The Apostle Paul taught, "Husbands, love your wives, even as Christ also loved the church, and gave himself for it."[1] Paul also taught, "Let the husband

---

1 Ephesians 5:25.

render unto the wife due benevolence: and likewise also the wife unto the husband."[2] We see the principles of kindness, respect, charity, care, and concern taught in these verses. Doug has previously written, "Remember that you are given your sexual capacities to bless your spouse, not for personal gratification alone. If a spirit of concern for the well-being of your spouse pervades your honeymoon—if you allow your body to be the instrument of joy for your spouse—you will both come away blessed."[3] Kindness, tenderness, respect, and concern should be the guiding principles for your honeymoon. This time can be a wonderful opportunity to cleave unto a spouse and quite literally become one.[4]

Explanation

Once married, sexual intimacy becomes a significant part of your romantic life together. There is a natural excitement that accompanies a couple's first venture into this intimate realm, especially the short time before the honeymoon when the level of anticipation is extremely high. Feelings intensify as the wedding reception comes to an end and you realize that you are about to have sex for the first time. For nearly every couple, the honeymoon can be a thrilling way to begin your intimate lives together. Remember, "a honeymoon is not about sexual performance as much as it is about the beginnings of sexual exploration, and simply getting to know each other in a more complete way."[5]

Despite the thrilling opportunity to get away on a honeymoon together, not every first sexual experience is spectacular. There are some couples who have difficulty "consummating the marriage" in their first attempts. In fact, the percentage of couples who have difficulty with sex the first time and even in subsequent attempts is surprisingly high. The key is to communicate with your partner and to focus on pleasure and being present in the moment, not on the outcome or result. As President Russell M. Nelson taught, "Husbands and wives, learn to listen, and listen to learn from one another. . . . Taking time to talk is essential to keep lines of communication intact. If marriage is a prime relationship in life, it deserves prime time!"[6] Couples who have healthy sex lives most often are good communicators. If there are sexual issues or concerns during the honeymoon, talk about it, discuss it, and try again. It is not a sign of failure; it is an opportunity to learn more about your partner and grow as a couple.

---

2   1 Corinthians 7:3.
3   S. E. Lamb & D. E. Brinley, *Between Husband & Wife* (2008), 52.
4   *See* Genesis 2:24.
5   D. M. Busby, J. S. Carroll, & C. Leavitt, *Sexual Wholeness in Marriage* (2013), 201.
6   Russell M. Nelson, "Listen to Learn," *Ensign*, May 1991, 22.

In our modern era, with television, movies, and social media saturating our society with sexual images and themes, it is easy to assume that today's couples know what to expect when they have sex for the first time on their wedding night. Perhaps some newly married individuals will assume that "nature will take its course." However, many couples soon learn that sex is not at all like the movies. So, how does a couple prepare to have sex for the first time on their wedding night and, subsequently, for their first sexual experiences on their honeymoon?

Again, communication is paramount, as couples should discuss with one another their expectations regarding the honeymoon and physical intimacy. Setting realistic expectations helps ease the pressure, and it increases clarity regarding individual sexual desires. Some things you may want to discuss include the following: How often would you like to have sex on your honeymoon? What do you imagine your wedding night to be like? What would you like to try? Is there anything you might feel uncomfortable doing or that is off-limits? How would you communicate what you are comfortable or uncomfortable doing? It is important to note that sex will not necessarily be an everyday occurrence during the week of the honeymoon. However, make intimacy—both emotional and physical—a priority during your honeymoon, and it will become a very special bonding experience that you will cherish.

Practical Application

At times, Latter-day Saint couples may inquire about what the Church says about how to prepare for a honeymoon or what is acceptable regarding the sexual relationship during your honeymoon and thereafter. We should be clear that the Church does not teach anything regarding honeymoons any more than the Church would give recommendations on where to take your car for an oil change. These are personal and private matters, and the Church is not going to intervene at this level of our lives. However, there are many things that we could consider best practices or, at least, recommended practices when it comes to these matters. We have already provided some counsel previously in this book; nevertheless, let us explore the honeymoon more specifically.

Preparing for the Wedding Night and Honeymoon:
Schedule a Pelvic Exam: For the bride-to-be, it is important to schedule a pelvic exam with your family doctor or an obstetrician/gynecologist (OB-GYN) before you get married. This is an opportunity to discuss birth-control options and make sure your body is ready for a healthy sexual relationship. "The pelvic exam is often a source of great anxiety for young women, especially those who have not been sexually active before. However, if

done carefully and sensitively, a pelvic exam should not be painful and usually involves only minor (if any) discomfort."[7]

Prevent Urinary Tract Infections (UTIs): A UTI is a bacterial bladder infection that women may contract after having sexual intercourse. Sometimes nicknamed "honeymoon cystitis," this infection is treated easily with antibiotics, but the symptoms include the urge to urinate frequently and painful urination. New brides can help prevent this infection by emptying the bladder before and after sexual relations, drinking plenty of water, and drinking cranberry juice.[8]

Get Sleep: We recommend that you have adequate sleep the night before your wedding day—it is going to be a long day, full of memorable moments, wedding festivities, spiritual experiences, pictures, and greeting your guests. You will want to be able to enjoy it all! Some individuals make the mistake of staying up too late the night before their wedding and then become exhausted on their wedding night. A lack of sleep can affect hormones, arousal, and overall physical intimacy on your wedding night and honeymoon; therefore, it is wise to get plenty of rest.

Make Time to Eat: Your wedding day will be extremely busy, and many couples do not set aside adequate time to eat. Much of their time is spent greeting wedding guests, attending to upcoming wedding festivities, and enjoying the moment! Numerous couples report eating very little of the food they chose to enjoy on their wedding day. We recommend having a family member or wedding coordinator box up food from the reception to take back to the hotel or have a plan to order food once you arrive. Fueling your body throughout your wedding day allows you to have the energy to enjoy it and to enjoy each other in the bedroom at the end of the night. Additionally, a special moment can be shared between husband and wife as they reminisce on their favorite memories of the wedding day while eating the food they picked out for their reception. Increasing emotional intimacy in this way can also help with physical intimacy later.

Bring Intimate Supplies: Physical arousal and stimulation increases vaginal lubrication, making sexual intercourse easier and more pleasurable for both partners. Without lubrication, sex can be uncomfortable and, at times, painful. Therefore, most women find it helpful to use an artificial lubricant for the first-time sexual experiences and any time they may experience vaginal

---

7 R. F. Stahmann, W. R. Young, & J. G. Grover, *Becoming One: Intimacy in Marriage* (2004), 23.
8 S. E. Lamb & D. E. Brinley, *Between Husband & Wife* (2000), 52.

dryness. Lubrication (also known as "lube") reduces friction during sex and can be water-based, oil-based, or silicone-based. Each of these options has pros and cons, and you will need to decide which one is right for you. Remember that lubrication is not a form of contraception, and again, birth control is something you and your partner need to address before the wedding night.

Set the Mood: Increasing romance and decreasing nerves on your wedding night can be accomplished by setting the right mood for intimacy. Atmosphere and ambiance can help draw your attention away from overthinking the moment to being present in the experience. Couples might want to take a bath or shower together to freshen up and to relax before physical intimacy. Be aware of your own personal hygiene and make efforts to be clean, apply a fragrance, and freshen up your breath. Wearing lingerie, lighting candles, eating chocolate-covered strawberries, placing rose petals on the bed, playing music in the background, and giving each other a massage are all ways to help set the mood for connection and romance.

Maintain Realistic Expectations: Not every sexual experience will be perfect or exactly what you had imagined. Be flexible, have a sense of humor, and adjust your expectations along the way. There may be a bit of miscommunication or small mishaps that you cannot avoid. One newlywed couple told us that the bride changed into lingerie, and while coming out of the bathroom, she tripped and stumbled onto the bed. The couple laughed it off, and it eased the pressure both newlyweds were feeling in that moment. Remember to keep it fun and lighthearted so you can enjoy your intimate time together.

Go Slow: We know it feels like you have been waiting forever, but there is no need to rush here. You will have the rest of your lives to be physically intimate together. Let things naturally happen, be gentle, and relax. Allow for the physical exploration of each other and focus on foreplay. In addition, listen to your body, read your partner's signals, communicate, and give yourself time to heat up. Some couples choose to sneak off to be together between the wedding ceremony and the reception or head to the hotel between wedding events. Just make sure that you allow yourself adequate time to enjoy your first sexual experiences together. Sometimes, it is better to wait for the right moment. Other couples schedule too much travel time or too many activities during their honeymoon. Slow down and truly get to know each other intimately during this time away together.

All in all, every couple's honeymoon should be unique and special to them. A honeymoon requires your time, but not necessarily every penny that you have ever earned. Just as you had a budget for the wedding ring, and the wedding itself, you should not focus on spending an exorbitant amount on the cost of the trip, but instead focus on the time together. The honeymoon does not have to be expensive, nor does it have to be in a far-away or exotic location. Make the best decision together as a couple regarding what your honeymoon should look like and cost. Nevertheless, we do recommend going on a honeymoon soon after the wedding, as it sets a positive tone for your married life.

Finally, it's vital to make a commitment to unplug, unwind, and focus on each other to increase connection during your honeymoon. The honeymoon is a couple's time away from outside distractions and other duties and responsibilities. You may want to leave your phone in the room, turn off your notifications, set aside a specific time to check social media or answer emails, and "go off the grid" as much as possible. Treasure this time together, and challenge yourself to be present for it. You only get one honeymoon, so make it special and make it count.

Question #9:
What do I need to know about birth control?

Among Latter-day Saints, there are many opinions about birth control. Some members are uncomfortable using birth control, while others use a variety of birth-control methods with no hesitation at all. Even so, it's important to understand the different types of birth control and use the method that best suits you. Several years ago, a woman told Mark's wife, "My husband and I *do not* practice birth control." Her tone seemed to condemn those who do use birth-control methods. Nevertheless, this woman had three children and had been married for over twenty years. Now, we do not claim to be rocket scientists or even obstetricians; however, barring any fertility issue, this woman was most likely using some form of birth control—otherwise, she would have had many more children over a twenty-year span of marriage. Indeed, avoiding a sexual relationship or only having sexual relationships during certain times of each month are also forms of birth control. Therefore, find what works best for you as a couple and leave the judgment of others around this topic at the door.

Principle

The Savior taught, "It is not meet that I should command in all things; for he that is compelled in all things, the same is a slothful and not a wise servant. . . . Men should be anxiously engaged in a good cause, and do many things of their own free will, and bring to pass much righteousness."[1] This verse of scripture implies that couples can make their own decisions when it comes to personal issues, such as family planning and birth control.

As members of The Church of Jesus Christ of Latter-day Saints, some of the deepest principles in our theology center on marriage and parenthood. We believe strongly in the family, and we are passionate that family life is the

---

1 Doctrine and Covenants 58:26–27.

core of human happiness. From *The Family: A Proclamation to the World*, the following doctrines are declared:

- "Marriage between a man and a woman is ordained of God and that the family is central to the Creator's plan for the eternal destiny of His children."
- "The first commandment that God gave to Adam and Eve pertained to their potential for parenthood as husband and wife. We declare that God's commandment for His children to multiply and replenish the earth remains in force."
- "We further declare that God has commanded that the sacred powers of procreation are to be employed only between man and woman, lawfully wedded as husband and wife."[2]

Elder Neil L. Andersen further explained, "This commandment [to bear children] has not been forgotten or set aside in The Church of Jesus Christ of Latter-day Saints. We express deep gratitude for the enormous faith shown by husbands and wives (especially our wives) in their willingness to have children. *When to have a child and how many children to have are private decisions to be made between a husband and wife and the Lord. These are sacred decisions—decisions that should be made with sincere prayer and acted on with great faith.*"[3]

Explanation

In the new and updated Church Handbook, birth control is addressed. The guideline on birth control states, "It is the privilege for married couples who are able to bear children to provide mortal bodies for the spirit children of God, whom they are responsible to nurture and rear. . . . The decision about how many children to have and when to have them is extremely personal and private. It should be left between the couple and the Lord."[4]

Church leaders are clearly emphasizing that birth control should be a private decision and one that is inclusive of prayer and spiritual guidance from the Lord. Due to personal revelation and the fact that each couple is different, there will be a wide variety in what birth-control options couples choose or do not choose in planning for their family.

We recognize that raising a family requires much time, energy, strength, sacrifice, patience, and love. Indeed, parenting can be challenging. We

---

2   "The Family: A Proclamation to the World," ChurchofJesusChrist.org.
3   Neil L. Andersen, "Children," *Ensign* or *Liahona*, Nov. 2011, 28; emphasis added.
4   *General Handbook: Serving in The Church of Jesus Christ of Latter-day Saints*, 38.6.4, ChurchofJesusChrist.org.

undoubtedly recommend receiving guidance and direction from our Father in Heaven on this particularly important matter and then moving forward with faith. Certainly, among newly married couples, it is wise to have some time to strengthen and develop the physical, spiritual, and emotional relationship before bringing children into the world. For some couples, they may need several years to develop their relationship properly, while other couples do not need as much time for such marital adjustments; therefore, each couple's situation may impact their choice regarding if and when to bring a baby into the world. This is why it is so important to involve the Lord in your decision—each couple is unique. There is not a one-size-fits-all answer. Many years ago, Elder Marion G. Romney testified,

> Now, I tell you that you can make every decision in your life correctly if you can learn to follow the guidance of the Holy Spirit. . . . Study your problems and prayerfully make a decision. Then take that decision and say to him, in a simple, honest supplication, 'Father, I want to make the right decision. I want to do the right thing. This is what I think I should do: let me know if it is the right course.' Doing this, you can get the burning in your bosom, if your decision is right. If you do not get the burning, then change your decision and submit a new one. *When you learn to walk by the Spirit, you never need to make a mistake.*[5]

The Lord will help you and your spouse know the path that you should pursue regarding birth control and growing your family. He will not only inspire you to do what is right for you as a married couple, but also what is right for your future children.

Practical Application

We would emphasize that you should be prayerful and discuss birth-control measures *before* you get married. In addition, you should also be flexible and adjust to the type of birth-control methods that work best for you and your spouse after marriage, since the ones you may try might not be a good fit after all. Here are some common birth-control methods to consider:

1. *Birth-Control Pill* (oral contraception): The pill is one of the most common methods of birth control for women. It is a medication that

---

5 Marion G. Romney, in Conference Report, Oct. 1961, 60–61; emphasis added.

comes in a monthly supply pack, and one pill is taken daily. The pill is prescribed by a doctor and is very safe and cost-efficient; however, it must be taken regularly to be effective. There are many types of birth-control pills; therefore, you may want to do your own research and consult with your OB-GYN on which birth-control pill is best for you. Moreover, as with any medication, there are possible side effects.

2. *Condoms:* A condom is a thin latex sheath that fits over a man's penis and prevents sperm from entering into the woman's body. Condoms are the most common "barrier" birth-control method, and perhaps the least expensive. They are easy to use, and most grocery stores and pharmacies carry them. Additionally, condoms are the only form of birth control that prevents sexually transmitted infections as well as prevents pregnancy.

3. *Intrauterine Device (IUD):* An IUD is a small, T-shaped device that is inserted into a woman's uterus by a doctor or nurse practitioner. The IUD prevents egg fertilization by changing how sperm cells move, thereby inhibiting conception. It is a long-term solution, very effective, and low maintenance. For a woman to conceive, the IUD is removed by her doctor. There are many different brands and types of IUDs, so it would be wise to research the options and consult with your doctor on the best IUD that may be right for you.

4. *Birth-Control Shot:* The birth-control shot works similarly to the birth-control pill. Both prevent ovulation in women and are safe and effective. However, the birth-control shot is administered every three months by a doctor, and it typically requires an appointment.

5. *Birth-Control Patch:* The birth-control patch is a thin patch placed on a woman's body to prevent pregnancy. The patch releases hormones that stop ovulation, and it is very effective as long as a woman changes it in a timely manner.

6. *Birth-Control Implant:* The birth-control implant is a tiny, thin rod that is inserted under the skin of a woman's upper arm. It releases a hormone to prevent pregnancy, and it lasts up to five years. Similar to the IUD, a doctor or nurse removes it when a woman wants to get pregnant.

7. *Internal Condom, Diaphragm, Cervical Cap, and the Sponge:* The internal condom is a soft plastic pouch a woman places inside her vagina as a covering of the cervix to prevent sperm from fertilizing an egg. A diaphragm works in the same way and is a shallow, bendable cup. The Cervical Cap is smaller than the diaphragm but is also shaped like a

dish and can stay in longer (up to two days). Additionally, a sponge is a soft, round, sponge-like material that is inserted into the vagina, blocking sperm from entering the uterus as well.

8. *Spermicide:* Spermicide is a chemical placed in the vagina (or on other birth-control methods, such as the diaphragm or cervical cap) to block the entrance to the cervix and to stop the movement of sperm so it does not fertilize the egg. It comes in different forms, such as creams, gels, film, foams, and suppositories.

9. *Fertility Awareness:* Fertility awareness refers to a woman tracking her menstruation cycle to know when she ovulates, thereby avoiding sex during ovulation or using other forms of birth control, such as condoms, during ovulation. However, this method alone is not as effective as other birth-control options. Nevertheless, practicing fertility awareness is very natural and does not require additional birth-control supplies. In addition, there are no side effects from medications or additional hormones.

10. *Withdrawal:* Withdrawal, also known as the "pull-out method," refers to a man pulling his penis out of the vagina before ejaculation. The goal is to prevent semen from entering the woman's vagina, thereby preventing pregnancy. This method is not as effective either because it can be difficult to be consistent, and if any semen enters the vagina at all, there is a risk of pregnancy. But again, this method does not involve any needed birth-control supplies or any side effects from medication or hormones.

It is typical for couples to try different forms of birth control before finding the one that works best for them. For example, some women choose to take the birth-control pill, and this practice works wonderfully for them. However, there are other women who become ill while taking the pill, or it affects them in adverse ways, such as weight gain, nausea, mood changes, a low libido (sexual desire), or perhaps even feelings of depression. For these women, they should consider other methods of birth control. As we have stated before, couples need to discuss what birth-control methods will work best for both of them. Perhaps the husband will need to be more involved in the birth-control practice, or both partners may have to take precautions.

The Savior taught, "For which of you, intending to build a tower, sitteth not down first, and counteth the cost, whether he have sufficient to finish it?"[6] And, likewise, "For which of you, intending to have a family, sitteth not down

---

6   Luke 14:28.

first, and counteth the cost, and considereth a host of other variables before you become pregnant and have a child?"

When it comes to bringing children into the world, there are many factors that should be considered, such as the emotional and physical health of the parents—especially the mother—as well as other factors, such as finances and emotional maturity.

Some newly married couples talk about "waiting to have children until they are ready." Be cautious about how you and your spouse define *ready*. Our experience is that if couples waited until they were truly ready, they may never have any children! Do not be afraid to move forward with faith if you are being spiritually guided to start your family. Additionally, if you want to *become* a great parent, you will need to seek the Lord's help, as well as your parents' help, and others who have experienced (and survived!) parenthood. We would encourage you to discover as much as you can about parenthood, and then put it into practice, giving yourself grace along the way. After all, no one can ever be completely ready for parenthood—at least, not by themselves. The Lord wants you to be parents, and He will help you along the way.

Question #10:
What if you had sex prior to marriage with someone else? Should you reveal this to your partner?

BECAUSE WE LIVE IN AN imperfect and fallen world—a world filled with sexual temptation and easy sexual access—there will be some who have experienced premarital sexual relations. All of us are grateful for the Atonement of Jesus Christ. Because of our Savior's sacrifice and love for us, we can repent of sexual transgressions and become clean. Nevertheless, premarital sexual experiences can affect marriage. Although many will certainly repent of their sexual transgressions, should a partner's sexual history be disclosed to their future spouse? Perhaps such choices occurred a long time ago. In some cases, perhaps before emotional maturity, self-control, spiritual strength, and self-discipline developed. What is the proper course to take if one is in this situation with their future spouse? During our time as professors and therapists, we have worked with many couples who have engaged in premarital sex. Even among active Church members, this has been a dilemma that couples must navigate and process. We have learned that, although it can be a challenge for couples to work through, premarital sexual intimacy does not have to be a "deal-breaker" that terminates a prospective marriage.

Principle

Intimacy in marriage is based on complete trust. President Harold B. Lee taught that a happy marriage must be built on the foundation of "love, trust, and faith."[1] Likewise, President James E. Faust explained, "Complete trust in each other is one of the greatest enriching factors in marriage."[2] There cannot be true intimacy and trust if there is not openness, truth, and disclosure. Moreover,

---

1 *Teachings of Harold B. Lee*, 251.
2 James E. Faust, "Enriching Your Marriage," *Ensign* or *Liahona*, Apr. 2007.

confidence cannot be established between couples if a partner is hiding sexual mistakes from the past—even if he or she has repented of them.

The Lord taught, "Behold, he who has repented of his sins, the same is forgiven, and I, the Lord, remember them no more. By this ye may know if a man repenteth of his sins—behold, he will confess them and forsake them."[3] We understand what it means to help someone through the repentance process. We know that the Atonement is real, and the vilest of sins can be washed clean. We also understand this statement from Richard G. Scott:

> If you, through poor judgment, were to cover your shoes with mud, would you leave them that way? Of course not. You would cleanse and restore them. Would you then gather the residue of mud and place it in an envelope to show others the mistake that you made? No. Neither should you continue to relive forgiven sin. Every time such thoughts come into your mind, turn your heart in gratitude to the Savior, who gave His life that we, through faith in Him and obedience to His teachings, can overcome transgression and conquer its depressing influence in our lives.[4]

Indeed, these are true principles. We recognize that no one needs to lay out their past sins out on the table for all to examine. If we have truly repented, we can keep our past sins to ourselves and move forward with faith. After all, if the Lord remembers our sins no more, then perhaps we should not dwell on them or be troubled by them either. However, marriage is not about one person; it is about two. When it comes to past sexual experiences, the individual you will marry deserves your utmost consideration and respect. Although it may be uncomfortable, their feelings and, frankly, their lives, must be considered. You cannot conceal information that is crucial to your partner's decision about marriage. Although individuals can repent of past mistakes, the impact of those choices still exists.

A person should be aware if their future spouse has been involved in addictions or other risks that could compromise a future marital union. We continue to meet couples who feel they were deceived into their marriages—the husband or wife did not reveal past sexual activity or a previous pornography addiction until after the marriage ceremony. A recent research study examined

---

3   Doctrine and Covenants 58:42–43.
4   Richard G. Scott, "We Love You—Please Come Back," *Ensign*, May 1986, 12.

the honesty of its participants regarding their disclosure of sexual histories with their partners. As high as 60 percent of participants admitted to deceiving their partner at some point when disclosing prior sexual experiences.[5] Deception is hurtful and can be devastating to your spouse. In many cases, lies and deception can be more damaging than the previous sins. Couples fare much better dealing with private, delicate information—such as past sexual activity of any kind—when the information is proactively shared rather than concealed and withheld to be inadvertently discovered later. Deception and lies destroy trust; transparency and openness build trust—it is that simple.

Explanation

We have seen the devastating effects when a spouse finds out later about their partner's previous sexual transgressions. They often wonder, "If they did not tell me about this in the beginning, what else are they hiding from me?" Such deception severely weakens the foundation of trust and creates many doubts and worries in the other spouse.[6] Many heartbroken couples in our counseling offices do not fully comprehend the significant correlation between dishonesty and trust and how it can destroy their relationship. All couples should strive for openness, honesty, and transparency in their relationships.

Elder Robert D. Hales used an analogy from his professional business life to explain how important it is for couples to do their "homework" long before they marry each other. He explained that before "one corporation acquires another, it thoroughly researches the other firm's strengths and weaknesses and its compatibility with the host company's strategic vision and way of doing business. Bundled together, these research activities are commonly referred to as 'due diligence.'"[7] This is when the host company would research the other organization's lawsuits, personnel, problems, assets, and liabilities. Once this investigation is complete, the company is prepared to make a well-informed decision about acquiring the other organization. *The more thorough the "due diligence," the fewer surprises will emerge after the acquisition.* Elder Hales then explained, "Individuals considering marriage would be wise to conduct their own prayerful due diligence. . . . I sometimes wonder whether doing more homework when it comes to this critical decision would spare some Church

---

5   *See* S. M. Horan, "Further Understanding Sexual Communication: Honesty, Deception, Safety, and Risk," *Journal of Social and Personal Relationships*, 33, no. 4 (2013): https://doi.org/10.1177/0265407515578821.

6   Interview of Laura Brotherson, on Feb. 25, 2019; notes in author's possession.

7   Robert D. Hales, *Return: Four Phases of Our Mortal Journey Home* (2010), 231.

members needless heartache. I fear too many fall in love with each other or even with the idea of marriage before doing the background research necessary to make a good decision."[8]

Using Elder Hales's metaphor, couples should also be thorough in their "due diligence" when it comes to prior moral issues, addictions, and transgressions. We all have weaknesses; we are all imperfect; we all sin. Elder Dieter F. Uchtdorf explained that we should be careful about judging others who simply sin differently than we do.[9]

So, when doing our due diligence before marriage, it need not be an interrogation or a demand for *specific* details. An individual would simply explain, "Several years ago, I had a pornography addiction. I worked through it with my bishop and a professional counselor. When I served my mission, I had no problems at all, and since that time, I have been free of the problem." Another could declare, "Before I met you, I was sexually active with my boyfriend. I confessed my sins to my bishop, and I have repented of those mistakes." Once again, there is no need to express the vivid details of a transgression that has been properly dealt with; however, the person you are planning to marry should know your sexual history—if you have one. *That is only fair to them.*

A sexual history includes any sexual activity prior to marriage, including sexual relationships with the opposite sex (or the same sex), masturbation, and pornography involvement. It would also be important to share with your partner if you have experienced any sexual abuse of any kind. Each of these can have a negative effect on a marriage, including shame, trauma, insecurities, fears, comparisons, unhealthy sexual conditioning, sexual dysfunctions, and sexual addictions. It is important that individuals be honest with their partners so those partners will be able to choose for themselves as to whether a particular relationship is right for them or not.

Several years ago, one of our students shared the following experience. Her sister had married a returned missionary while they were both students at Brigham Young University. This woman had every reason to believe that her returned missionary husband was worthy and faithful. However, about a year after their marriage, he reengaged himself in a serious pornography addiction. This man eventually revealed to his new bride that he had actually been addicted to pornography since early adolescence. He also disclosed that he had been sexually active while in high school and college. After marriage, his addiction continued until his sexual deviance escalated into many

---

8   Robert D. Hales, *Return*, 232–233.
9   *See* Dieter F. Uchtdorf, "The Merciful Obtain Mercy," *Ensign* or *Liahona*, May 2012.

extramarital affairs with multiple partners. Although he eventually shared this devastating information with his wife, the damage was irreparable, and it was too late to save the marriage.

The student who was relating this experience reported that her sister was now divorced. This woman now lived as a single mother in an apartment with four young children. She works a meager job, and her children spend most of their time at a daycare center. The student then shared the following with great emphasis: "Had my sister known that her husband was a sexual addict, and had a sordid sexual past, she would have never married him in the first place. Now she lives a very difficult life, all because a man did not reveal issues from his past. This is a marriage that could have been avoided."

Some individuals adhere to the theory that the only "intimate" thing they can know about their future spouse is whether they hold a current temple recommend. May we suggest that there are many additional things you should know about your future spouse. After all, you will be linking your life to this individual for all eternity. You have the right to know everything about that person, and they have the right to know everything about you. Marrying someone for eternity is a huge commitment and investment.

Practical Application

Once you have determined that you are serious with the person you are dating, and it appears that you may be discussing engagement and marriage, it is certainly the right time to have an open, honest, and frank discussion regarding any past sexual activity. You should be able to ask each other questions like the following:

- Have you ever had a sexual relationship (including oral sex) with another person?
- Have you ever experienced sexual abuse or trauma of any kind?
- Have you ever touched someone else sexually without their consent?
- Have you ever been sexually attracted to someone of the same sex?
- Have you every masturbated before, and what are your thoughts/feelings about masturbation?
- What kind of exposure have you had to pornography? What difficulties or issues have you noticed as a result?
- If you have not been able to overcome pornography or other sexual issues on your own, have you worked with a trained professional counselor or therapist on recovery?

- Have you ever tested positive for a sexually transmitted infection?
- If you have had sexual experiences in the past, have you repented and worked with priesthood leaders on resolving them?
- Is there anything else in your sexual past that I should be aware of?

Questions such as these, asked in the right tone, with a loving attitude and with the proper intent, can invite wonderful discussions where the Holy Ghost can attend. In fact, from our experience in counseling couples, revealing past sexual experiences has rarely been a deal-breaker. Instead, where there have been sexual issues in the past for one of the partners, most of the couples we have counseled eventually moved forward and were ultimately married in the temple. Yes, there were issues that had to be worked through, but once the problems were resolved, these couples prepared themselves for marriage in the temple. Perhaps even more important, these couples established a practice of open communication in their relationships and built a stronger foundation of trust in their marriage.

Being transparent about previous sexual experiences can help create a culture in your future marriage of full disclosure for the rest of your lives. It can prepare you to be honest and open about everything—which is what true intimacy is all about. These couples work as a team, they enjoy recreational companionship, they plan their futures together, they laugh together, they cry together, and in essence—they share a meaningful, rich, joyous life as husband and wife.

Question #11:
Is there any advice you could give to those of us who have a fiancé(e) who has been a victim of sexual molestation/abuse?

IN THE UNITED STATES, EVERY nine minutes, a child is sexually abused, and over 65,000 children are abused each year.[1] This statistic is startling and unimaginable. It also speaks to how many couples are affected by childhood abuse; in fact, if you or your partner have been abused, you are not alone. While trauma and abuse can affect the marital relationship, survivors of childhood sexual abuse can have healthy partnerships and healthy sex lives. But it is not surprising that it may come with some external help and support.

First and foremost, be informed about what sexual abuse is and how it affects your partner specifically. For example, not all abuse occurs in childhood. Sometimes, abuse can take place during adolescent and the young-adult years. The two types of sexual abuse include touching and non-touching. Touching consists of touching a person's private parts, making an individual touch the private parts of someone else, or penetration of private parts with an object or another person's body parts for sexual pleasure. Non-touching abuse occurs by showing pornography to a child, exposing one's private parts to a child/adult, prostituting/trafficking a child/adult, photographing a child in sexual poses, encouraging a child to watch or hear sexual acts either in person or on a video, and/or watching a child/adult undress or use the bathroom.[2] Unfortunately, there are individuals who are sexually abused as a child, youth, or even as an adult. Studies verify that 20 percent of adult women and 5 to 10 percent of adult men can recall a childhood sexual assault or sexual abuse incident in their lives.[3]

---

1   *See* "About Child Sexual Abuse," *Prevent Child Abuse—North Carolina*, https://www.preventchildabusenc.org/resource-hub/about-child-sexual-abuse/.
2   *See* "About Child Sexual Abuse."
3   *See* "Child Sexual Abuse Statistics," *The National Center for Victims of Crime*, https://victimsofcrime.org/child-sexual-abuse-statistics/.

Additionally, sexual abuse can have long-term effects on a person, including impeding one's sexual relationship as an adult. But the impact is far more reaching than that. Adult survivors of childhood sexual abuse are three times more likely to experience depression and four times more likely to suffer from post-traumatic stress disorder or PTSD.[4] Other effects of sexual abuse are self-blame, self-esteem issues, anxiety, addiction, violence, promiscuity, and suicidal thoughts.[5] Thus, the trauma and recovery from childhood sexual abuse not only impacts the survivor themselves but also the people they love.

Principle

Jesus Christ took upon Himself "the pains and the sicknesses of his people."[6] For those who have been sexually abused, there is hope in healing. The Savior is aware of your pain; He suffered that exact pain for you so that you could be freed from it. Jesus Christ knew that people would suffer this particular agony at the hands of others. He taught in the scriptures that, "whoso shall offend one of these little ones which believe in me, it were better for him that a millstone were hanged about his neck, and that he were drowned in the depth of the sea."[7] Experts estimate that a small millstone could weigh well over 1,000 pounds. This metaphor helps even the casual scripture reader understand the Savior's poignant feelings toward those who abuse His children.

The Atonement of Jesus Christ is the answer for healing, cleansing, and renewing. Our Savior and Redeemer will heal the brokenhearted, the bruised, battered, and torn. Tad Callister wrote,

> There is a miraculous rebirth, a spiritual phoenix that emerges with our acceptance of the Savior and His Atonement. His spirit heals; it refines; it comforts; it breathes new life into hopeless hearts. It has the power to transform all that is ugly and vicious and worthless in life into something of supreme and glorious splendor. He has the power to convert the ashes of mortality to the beauties of eternity.[8]

---

4   *See* RAINN, "Children and Teens: Statistics," https://www.rainn.org/statistics/children-and-teens.

5   *See* "When Your Partner Was Sexually Abused as a Child: A Guide for Partners," Sexual Abuse Information Series (2008), https://www.canada.ca/content/dam/phac-aspc/migration/phac-aspc/sfv-avf/sources/nfnts/nfnts-visac-partnr/assets/pdf/nfntsx-visac-partn_e.pdf.

6   Alma 7:11–12.

7   Matthew 18:6.

8   Tad R. Callister, *The Infinite Atonement* (2000), 206–207.

Any person who has experienced trauma in their life can be spiritually healed through the Savior and the Atonement of Jesus Christ. As couples work together to overcome these challenges, spouses have a profound opportunity to develop Christlike characteristics, such as patience, kindness, tenderness, strength, and empathy toward one another. Learning to turn to the Lord to access His enabling power to heal and help individuals and couples through these mortal challenges can be a great blessing. Couples can achieve a healthy and satisfying sexual relationship in their marriage by working as a team—not against each other—and, in many cases, with the assistance of a trusted and competent therapist.

Explanation

Sexual abuse is the ultimate form of betrayal. In fact, 93 percent of child sexual abuse occurs by someone the person knows and trusts.[9] Therefore, adult survivors of childhood sexual abuse often experience a lack of trust in relationships because someone they believed in completely took advantage of them for their own sexual gratification. In addition, survivors may feel like their partner is manipulating them in some way and question their spouse's motives. It is often hard to know whom to trust and what their agenda might be, even with loved ones. Thus, establishing trust will be particularly important to a married couple where one partner has experienced abuse as a child. Indeed, couples may choose to use a safe word when they need to stop talking about a particular topic, halt physical intimacy, or leave a certain situation that is triggering uncomfortable feelings or memories of the abuse. Open communication around the trauma helps to build trust between husband and wife.

Adult survivors of childhood sexual abuse also experience powerlessness. Their power was taken from them in a very traumatic way, and it is difficult for them to feel like they possess it again. At times, it can be tough to assert oneself and express personal needs and wants in a relationship or put boundaries in place and not allow others to walk all over them. Other times, such individuals may become quite controlling—feeling that they may be in danger if they do not manage and control every aspect of their lives and, in some cases, the lives of others.[10] Either way, powerlessness can lead to an inability to make decisions, self-destructive behaviors, and anger issues, and it can prove to be an arduous task to navigate for couples.

---

9   *See* RAINN, "Children and Teens: Statistics."
10 *See* "When Your Partner Was Sexually Abused as a Child," 3.

Another difficulty for adult survivors of childhood sexual abuse is emotional intimacy. Survivors often feel shame, as if the abuse was their fault. In truth, they are completely innocent and pure—they did nothing wrong. They are not to blame for any aspect of the abuse, and they are certainly not guilty of any sexual transgression. However, the shame can linger, prevent attachment, and encourage distance from others. Abuse survivors often learn to "block out" or shut off their emotions as a coping mechanism. A person may keep a wall up, not allowing their partner to get too close out of fear of being hurt or deceived again. They may believe their partner's needs are more important than their own, so they do not open up and share their wants and desires. Even more, they have difficulty experiencing positive emotions or the feelings of love from Heavenly Father. Thus, your partner would benefit from an increase in love, patience, nurturing, and reassurance in your relationship. Build them up and validate their self-worth by treating them with kindness and respect, giving them compliments, and demonstrating complete acceptance of who they are as your spouse.

Regarding sexuality, adult survivors of childhood sexual abuse may not view their body as a source of pleasure, but instead, a source of discomfort. Sex is not necessarily associated with love, and such individuals may withdraw from sex at times. Some come to believe that attention and affection from their partner are purely indicators of sexual activity, so they disengage from that as well. With certain areas of the body, some may feel uneasy when touched, or others might require special circumstances, such as turning the lights off. In addition, there may be difficulty in arousal or orgasm. Others may be preoccupied with sex or have an excessive interest in it. The key is to be open and communicate how the effects from sexual abuse can impact your own intimate relationship.

Practical Application

So, if this traumatic experience can cause so much damage—why would sexual abuse survivors want to engage in such an act that caused so much heartache and trauma in their early life? One simple answer is that is a way a survivor regains their power and does not remain a victim. To enjoy their own sexuality and to share physical intimacy with their partner is how they can move forward and not allow the perpetrator to take anything else away from them. It is worth it; it might be a lot of work to get there, but healing is possible. Here are some ways you can help:

1. **Believe your partner who has endured the abuse.** Listen to your partner's story and validate their feelings about the past trauma.

Accept where your partner is currently at and understand how their sexual abuse affects them now. Be careful to not press your partner for specific details, and instead, allow your partner to share what they are comfortable with sharing. Know that recalling specific details of the abuse can be retraumatizing for your partner, so let your partner lead the way. As you articulate your belief in their story, it establishes trust in your relationship and increases emotional safety.

2. **Create space for healing.** Never tell your spouse who has been through childhood sexual abuse to "just move on" or "forgive and forget." We should never tell a person who has been diagnosed with a serious disease to "just put it behind you and move forward." Likewise, no one should ever tell a survivor of sexual abuse they should just forget their trauma and move ahead. These statements lack empathy and understanding. Most likely, the "non-abused" spouse does not understand the specific trauma and challenges the abused spouse has experienced. Instead, create space for your partner to heal. Allow them to feel okay in one moment and not okay in the next, because that's how trauma works. The healing process is not a linear one but more of a cycle of ups and downs.

3. **Identify and recognize prompts, cues, and triggers.** Be aware of words, locations, experiences, and situations that can be triggering for your spouse. One day, they may be completely fine, and then after viewing a television program, or after something was mentioned on social media, they may revert in their progression and even spiral downward. Triggers can activate post-traumatic stress symptoms, such as nightmares or sleep disturbances, dissociation, irritability, aggressiveness, hopelessness, or self-destructive behavior. In the blink of an eye, a good day can turn south. Be empathetic, listen to your partner, learn to recognize the triggers, and help your spouse cope with them.

4. **Be sensitive and respect boundaries.** When it comes to physical intimacy, it may be best to allow your partner to be in control of initiating sex and encourage them to tell you which sexual positions feel comfortable. Make sure to establish a pattern of verbal consent at each step along the way. If sexual activity triggers your partner in any way, try nonsexual touch and affection. Focus on pleasure instead of intercourse or solely achieving an orgasm. Moreover, be there for your partner and respect his or her boundaries, because as stated previously, boundaries may not be easy to put in place for an adult survivor of childhood sexual abuse.

5. **Find other non-physical ways to express your love.** Love can be expressed through physical touch but also through other love languages, such as acts of service, words of affirmation, quality time, and thoughtful gift-giving.[11] Take the love languages quiz online at www.5lovelanguages.com and find out how your partner feels loved. Then, focus on demonstrating your love in a non-physical way to your partner in order to strengthen your connection.
6. **Seek professional counseling.** Many adult survivors of childhood sexual abuse do not receive professional counseling help after the trauma has occurred. However, they should seek the help of a trained professional if they are currently experiencing traumatic symptoms or the trauma is affecting their relationships with loved ones. Others may have engaged in counseling after the abuse occurred but are experiencing trauma symptoms presently. That is an indication to go back to counseling and continue the work. Spouses should also be willing to attend counseling sessions to obtain the tools necessary to help their partner. Managing the effects of sexual abuse together can be extremely helpful to a couple and the healing journey.
7. **Rely on Jesus Christ.** The teachings, doctrines, and principles of the gospel of Jesus Christ can heal "the wounded soul."[12] Rely on Jesus Christ, the Atonement, and the teachings of the gospel that can help provide comfort and healing. Elder Richard G. Scott stated, "Complete healing will come through your faith in Jesus Christ and His power and capacity, through His Atonement, to heal the scars of that which is unjust and undeserved. . . . He loves you. He gave His life that you may be free of needless burdens. He will help you do it. I know that He has the power to heal you."[13]

Challenges that exist because of sexual abuse can be navigated; the effects from sexual abuse can be overcome. Individuals do not need to live their lives suffering in silence, drenched in shame, and smothered by the past. There is hope and healing for everyone. Our Savior, Jesus Christ, invites us to come unto Him, to cast our burdens at His feet, and to experience joy and healing *now*—not 100 years from now, or one day on the other side of the veil, but now. As couples work together, they can prevail over the wrongs of the past and create hope and healing in their marriages.

---

11 *See* Gary Chapman, *The 5 Love Languages: The Secret to Love that Lasts* (2015).
12 Jacob 2:8.
13 Richard G. Scott, "To Be Free of Heavy Burdens," *Ensign* or *Liahona*, Nov. 2002, 88.

Question #12:
What if you know you cannot have children? When should you tell your fiancé(e)?

We are acquainted with a man who was in a serious accident as a teenager. His pelvis was crushed during the trauma, and doctors told him that because internal damage had wreaked havoc on his body, he probably would not be able to father his own children. When he became serious with the girl he was dating, he disclosed the personal and private information to her. As she accepted the probability that they would not have any of their own biological children together, this couple chose to move forward with faith.

Any information that can affect your fiancé's future should be revealed long before your engagement or wedding day. Of course, this kind of information needs to be shared with a future spouse, but the primary question here is, "When is the right time?" Timing is crucial. You do not want to reveal a serious issue on the second date. However, you also should not wait until you are walking into the temple doors on your wedding day to reveal a serious matter.

Consider another example. We know another couple who encountered a unique dilemma. The man was a pediatric neurosurgeon who spent every day of his life dealing with young children and their life-threatening illnesses. He had to console brokenhearted parents, often informing them that the lifespan of their child would be much shorter than they expected. Because of the disturbing nature of his job, this man decided, after he had been married for several years, that he no longer wanted to have children of his own. However, his wife was a woman who wanted nothing more than to be a mother and raise a family. In this case, the timing of revealing his position to his wife proved challenging for their marriage and was extremely difficult to navigate.

Principle

Honesty and the timing of sensitive disclosures are both important to healthy relationships. Honesty is the foundation upon which trust is built, and trust is essential for a strong and healthy marriage. In Ecclesiastes we read, "To every thing there is a season, and a time to every purpose under heaven. . . . A time to keep silence, and a time to speak."[1] President Dallin H. Oaks declared, "In all the important decisions in our lives, what is most important is to *do the right thing*. Second, and only slightly behind the first, is to *do the right thing at the right time*. People who do the right thing at the wrong time can be frustrated and ineffective. They can even be confused about whether they made the right choice when what was wrong was not their choice but their timing."[2] Indeed, information such as the desire and ability to have children could affect your future spouse's decision to marry and should certainly be shared at the right time in the relationship.

Explanation

Latter-day Saints believe that marriage and family life continue beyond mortality. Therefore, the matter of having children is essential to address. President Dallin H. Oaks taught:

> Knowledge of God's plan for His children gives Latter-day Saints a unique perspective on marriage and family. We are correctly known as a family-centered church. . . . We know that the marriage of a man and a woman is necessary for the accomplishment of God's plan. Only this marriage will provide the approved setting for mortal birth and to prepare family members for eternal life. We look on marriage and the bearing and nurturing of children as part of God's plan and a sacred duty of those given the opportunity to do so.[3]

The scriptures teach that a husband and wife are commanded to "multiply and replenish the earth."[4] *The Family: A Proclamation to the World* states, "The first commandment that God gave to Adam and Eve pertained to their potential for parenthood as husband and wife. We declare that God's commandment for His children to multiply and replenish the earth remains in force."[5] In marriage, men and women have the opportunity to begin adding to their family through the wonderful privilege of procreation. However, there

---

1 Ecclesiastes 3:1, 7.
2 Dallin H. Oaks, "Timing" (Brigham Young University devotional, Jan. 29, 2002), speeches.bu.edu.
3 Dallin H. Oaks, "No Other Gods," *Ensign* or *Liahona*, Nov. 2013.
4 Genesis 1:28.
5 "The Family: A Proclamation to the World," ChurchofJesusChrist.org.

are couples who will have difficulty conceiving and bearing children of their own through reproductive issues, disease, injuries, or other health concerns.

Nevertheless, when should this information be shared with a potential spouse? The answer lies in that very word: *potential*. If the relationship grows and feelings of love begin, or the relationship has the potential to develop into marriage, then it is appropriate and necessary to disclose this information and discuss the ability and timing of having children with your significant other. Often this conversation should transpire long before talk of an engagement or wedding, but instead when you feel that the love you have for your significant other is beginning to blossom. This could be different for each couple. At this juncture, the relationship has a foundation of care, concern, trust, and respect. For some couples, this is early on in the relationship because feelings can start out very intensely. For other couples, the relationship develops slower and is more spread out over time. Moreover, long-distance relationships can also take more time to develop. Regardless, when feelings progress and you see potential for a future together, the relationship should be strong and sturdy enough to handle this kind of information.

The following experience was shared by a colleague, Dr. Sean Brotherson, a Latter-day Saint professor at North Dakota State University. A woman named Debbie, married for nineteen years, told Sean the following experience:

> I was head over heels in love with Peter and had been dating him for a couple of weeks when I realized how serious we were both feeling. I knew there was something I had to talk to him about but was afraid—would he leave me?
>
> I have multiple sclerosis and had been in and out of a wheelchair already (I was diagnosed at eighteen). I was afraid that once he found out I was "less than perfect" he would leave me for someone better. But we sat down together and I told him, knowing the possibilities.
>
> He turned to me, held my hand and looked into my eyes as he said, "Deb, if you are going to be in a wheelchair for the rest of your life, I am going to be there to push it." I knew I could never be with anyone else.
>
> Since then, I have been in and out of wheelchairs and he has been there to carry me and to push the chairs. . . . We have suffered our share of hardships, but we have done it all together and still look to our future together. I love him more

today than I did on the day I married him, and the first thing I do when I wake up is say a prayer of thanks to the Lord for my precious husband and my children.[6]

This experience highlights the need to share personal, intimate information in a healthy, constructive way. To withhold sensitive information from a prospective spouse would not be fair to either one of you. Information such as an inability to have children should be available to a potential partner who may or may not have a difficult time understanding and accepting such information.

Most of the time, the experience of sharing serious concerns with a potential partner goes surprisingly well. Why? Because couples who have feelings for one another have already established a pattern of transparency and openness, and they have practiced acceptance and tolerance. When couples develop feelings of love, there is not much information about each other that would cause them to terminate the relationship. Obviously, there are those who would want to end the relationship, but it is our experience that most people choose to hang in there when sensitive information is disclosed.

Moreover, we all must remember that the person we marry is going to have flaws—they will be imperfect—and so is each one of us! President Uchtdorf said, "One of the things I've realized as I've matured in life is that if someone is willing to accept me—as imperfect as I am—then I should be willing to be patient with others' imperfections as well. Since you won't find perfection in your partner, and your partner won't find it in you, your only chance at perfection is in creating perfection together."[7]

Practical Application

If you have something sensitive yet significant to tell the person that you are dating, such as that you can't bear children, don't want to have children, or that you have a health concern or some other significant issue you feel needs to be disclosed, reach out to them in faith. Here are some suggested guidelines for this discussion:

1. First, determine if the relationship has *potential*. If you are developing feelings that could lead to a future with this person, then it is important to be open and transparent with your partner on all issues. Also, if a

---

6 Debbie Kiss, "I Will Be There" in Sean E. Brotherson, "The Sweetest Love Stories," *Meridian Magazine*, May 4, 2012, https://ldsmag.com/article-1-9975/.

7 Dieter F. Uchtdorf, "The Reflection in the Water" (CES Devotional, Nov. 1, 2009), https://www.churchofjesuschrist.org/media/video/2009-11-0050-the-reflection-in-the-water?lang=eng.

dating partner asks you directly if you can have children, be honest in the moment—never hide it. Even if you feel it's a bit soon to be having the discussion, it's more important to establish a pattern of honesty from the very beginning.

2. Be comfortable with the issue (infertility or otherwise) and who you are. Make peace with it, accept its presence in your life, and release the shame associated with this issue. The National Infertility Association reports that one in eight couples have difficulty getting pregnant or maintaining pregnancy.[8] Therefore, recognize that other couples will struggle too and that you are not alone. The more comfortable you are with the information you are sharing, the more comfortable your partner will be when you discuss this sensitive information.

3. Choose an appropriate time and location to share your personal and private issue with your partner. It should be a time where you both are relaxed, free from distractions, and have time to discuss your thoughts and feelings on the subject.

4. Explain your situation and the challenges that accompany your circumstance. Talk "knee to knee and toe to toe," figuratively speaking. Open up, be honest, and share your deepest fears and how this issue has affected your life and those around you. You are not going to say everything right or perfectly, but share what is in your heart, and your partner will be there to receive it. It is okay to feel nervous or scared, but it is more important to feel vulnerable and authentic and provide an opportunity of connection in your relationship through a difficult issue. Give your partner a chance to be there for you.

5. Allow your partner to ask questions. Create an environment of kindness and respect as you respond to each other's concerns.

6. After you have disclosed the information to your partner, offer time and space for them to consider their thoughts and feelings regarding this new information.

7. Reconvene sometime after the information has been shared to check in with each other and gauge your thoughts and feelings. Know that this will not be the only discussion you have with your partner regarding this issue, but there will most likely be many discussions regarding the information you've shared. Be prepared and open to having additional conversations.

---

8 See "Facts, Diagnosis, and Risk Factors," Resolve: National Infertility Association; https://resolve.org/learn/infertility-101/facts-diagnosis-and-risk-factors/.

8. Include Heavenly Father in the process. Pray over the matter separately or possibly together if that feels appropriate. Seek divine guidance and direction as you navigate your way through this decision.

At this point, you and your partner will decide to reengage in the relationship and move forward with faith or discontinue your association for now. If the relationship ends, it will likely be very difficult. This will be one of those opportunities to trust in the Lord and His purposes for you, even when those purposes are not clear. It is better that you have this conversation and are both able to make a decision before the relationship progresses any further. You can trust in the Lord as you share and work through your challenges, knowing all things will work together for your good.[9]

---

9 *See* Doctrine and Covenants 105:40 and Romans 8:28.

Question #13:
What are some ways for couples to talk about their sexual relationship? How often should those conversations take place?

The song "Let's Talk about Sex" by Salt and Peppa was very popular in 1990. If truth be told, some of us can still recite every single line. The song was not only catchy, but its message was also important: "Let's talk about sex; let's talk about all the good things and the bad things that may be." The artists even sang about how you can turn the radio off, or press pause, but avoiding the discussion of sex will not stop people from having sex. Yet, when it comes to sex, it is much easier to do it than to talk about it. In fact, in the context of marriage, we even expect it to go perfectly without saying much or speaking a word at all. However, we need to be talking about sex outside the bedroom to get what we want inside the bedroom.

Thus, most books on sexual intimacy will include a chapter on communication. If LDS couples want to have a healthy sex life, they will need to discuss intimacy often. Several years ago, one of us saw a bumper sticker on the back of a pickup truck that read, "My wife says I don't listen to her or something like that." And therein lies the problem! When communicating about sensitive issues—especially sexual issues—husbands and wives will need to give their full attention to each other. In this case, listening is equally as crucial as speaking.

Healthy communication about the sexual dynamics of marriage should become a preeminent, regular practice. Although some couples may assume that a satisfying sexual relationship will occur organically, wise couples come to understand that communication and working together are key ingredients to happiness in general and sexual fulfillment. Unfortunately, many husbands and wives remain silent when it comes to their sex lives. Such silence can lead to feelings of hurt, resentment, frustration, and overall dissatisfaction.

Moreover, communication about sexual intimacy can serve as a preventive maintenance program to keep a marriage humming on all cylinders. Couples should not only address each other when there are problems, but should conduct regular check-ins, which can prevent small issues from becoming larger ones. Most of us already participate in regular medical checkups. We visit the dentist for a cleaning, even when our teeth are not giving us trouble. We have the oil in our cars changed about every 3–5,000 miles to keep the engine running. Unfortunately, most couples do not participate in this sort of preventive maintenance for their marriages. However, if couples make it a point to have regular couple meetings about their intimacy, among other things, they can avoid most of the common pitfalls that plague modern marriages.

Principle

When couples discuss sexual intimacy, they should follow the admonition of Paul, who said, "Let no corrupt communication proceed out of your mouth, but that which is good to the use of edifying, that it may minister grace unto the hearers."[1] Couples should counsel together with love and a desire to understand their sexual differences, desires, and challenges. What you say and how you say it is of utmost importance.

Dr. Stephen R. Covey believed that communication was the most important skill in life. In his book *Seven Habits of Highly Effective People*, Dr. Covey taught, seek first to understand and then to be understood. Developing a habit of seeking first to understand your spouse before voicing your own thoughts and opinions is especially important if you tend to be the more-expressive partner. Dr. Covey believed that most people listen with an intent to reply, not to understand. He pointed out that people want to make their point; thereby, they may ignore their partner, pretend they are listening, selectively hear only parts of the conversation, or miss the meaning entirely. Instead, people need to practice empathic listening, which involves seeing the world as your partner sees it so you can truly understand how they feel.[2]

As mentioned in a previous chapter, reflective listening is a useful tool for couples to implement when it comes to communication. When your partner expresses their thoughts and feelings, reflect back to him or her what you heard your partner say. This allows your partner to feel heard, to know that you understand their point of view, and to share more with you. You might try to role-play as well. Pretend you are each other, and try to convey the message you feel your partner is saying. It can be eye-opening to hear your own words

---

1   Ephesians 4:29; emphasis added.
2   *See* Stephen R. Covey, *The 7 Habits of Highly Effective People* (2004).

directed back at yourself, and when you must put yourself in your partner's shoes, you truly learn to empathize.

Paul taught, "And be ye kind one to another, tenderhearted, forgiving one another, even as God for Christ's sake hath forgiven you."[3] As the Apostle implied, discussing physical intimacy requires tenderness, care, and respect on the part of both companions. This can be a difficult topic to discuss initially after marriage because of one's inexperience in talking with a member of the opposite sex about anatomy or the use of sexual terms as you discover your own sexuality with your spouse. However, it is essential to gain the necessary tools as you begin your physical relationship and establish safety and trust when talking about sex.

Explanation

The answer to the question "How should couples talk about sex?" is quite simple. Many years ago, Elder Marvin J. Ashton declared, "If we would know true love and understanding one for another, we must realize that communication is more than a sharing of words. It is the *wise* sharing of emotions, feelings, and concerns. It is the sharing of oneself totally."[4] Thus, marital communication regarding physical intimacy should be more than words—emotions also must be discussed and processed. Brigham Young University professors Busby, Carroll, and Leavitt explained:

> Above all, marriage research stresses the need for couples to pay attention to their communication patterns, and to be willing to work at improving authentic and healthy communication skills. At its roots, effective sexual communication is how well spouses listen to each other—with their hearts as well as their ears—and openly divulge their sexual needs and desires. Over time, a couple's relationship will either be strengthened through the presence of—or eroded by the absence of—effective sexual communication. Such patient listening can cultivate true intimacy, heal hurts, and strengthen the sense of partnership. When you communicate in this way, your spouse is much more likely to trust you, thus opening the door for

---

3 Ephesians 4:32.
4 Marvin J. Ashton, "Family Communications," *Ensign*, May 1976, 52.

ongoing intimate communications and more positive sexual interactions.[5]

For communication regarding physical intimacy to be effective, it must penetrate the heart of each partner because of its personal and vulnerable nature. Talking about the sexual relationship within marriage needs to be Christlike, loving, respectful, soft, and tender. Yelling, criticizing, accusing, finger-pointing, or even giving the silent treatment will never motivate a spouse to communicate more with their partner; rather, it silences them. To help couples communicate more effectively when it comes to sex, we put together a Dos and Don'ts list:

Dos
1. Talk about sex early on, even before marriage and certainly on your honeymoon and thereafter.
2. Take responsibility for your own pleasure by expressing desires to your spouse.
3. Clarify your own thoughts before you talk to your spouse about your sexual relationship.
4. Make clear statements to avoid confusion.
5. Use "I" statements, and avoid starting any conversation with "you."
6. Recognize the positive, and affirm your spouse.
7. Find the humor in sex (humor decreases tension and increases relaxation).
8. Say "yes" to what you want and "no" to what you don't.
9. Pay attention to non-verbal communication (body movements, breathing, auditory cues).
10. Make suggestions instead of complaints.

Don'ts
1. Do not talk about sexual issues right after sex; give your spouse time and space first, and then talk about it outside the bedroom.
2. Do not compromise or do something you do not want to do. This leads to resentment and disconnection.
3. Do not phrase something as a question. Instead phrase it as a statement. ("Can we try something different?" vs. "I would like to try something different.") This leads to an open-ended conversation instead of a yes-or-no answer.

---

5 Dean M. Busby, Jason S. Carroll, & Chelom Leavitt, *Sexual Wholeness in Marriage: An LDS Perspective on Integrating Sexuality and Spirituality in our Marriages* (2013), 123–124.

4. Do not fake an orgasm, as this tells your partner to keep doing something that is not working for you.
5. Do not be negative or critical of your partner's performance. Instead, discuss what is working for you or what isn't.
6. Don't expect your spouse to read your mind or assume your spouse knows what you want without talking.
7. Do not post about your sex life on social media or reveal personal details to your friends, as that affects trust with your partner and will severely affect your communication regarding sex.
8. Do not get defensive, because when you defend yourself, you aren't listening. Be receptive to feedback.
9. Do not text about it; TALK about it. Have confidence that you and your spouse can gain the skills to talk about sex even though it may be difficult at times. Resist addressing hard topics through *only* texting or emailing. A text or email might start the conversation, but it is important to follow up in person.
10. Do not be resistant to professional counseling if you find that you and your spouse are struggling to talk about sex.

Practical Application

Couples who talk about sex have better relationships because good communication lends to more understanding and clarity of your partner's feelings. Also, a couple's desires and expectations regarding the sexual relationship will certainly be fluid, and changes over the course of your life will need to be addressed. Therefore, constant communication about the sexual relationship will be essential for both marital and sexual satisfaction.

One helpful intervention could be a regular, consistent couple's meeting. Couple's meetings work best when kept brief and, of course, positive. A surefire way to kill a couples meeting is to drag it out for hours and to metaphorically club each other over the head with marital issues. We recommend you meet at the same time each week. Begin this meeting with a prayer to invite the Spirit and to begin the conversation in a meaningful way. Consider the following agenda items:

- Review your schedules for the week, and coordinate your activities.
- Briefly review your weekly finances, goals, and budget items.
- Review any couple or family problems that need to be addressed.
- Review family goals and couple goals.
- Plan and schedule your couple time and date night for the week.

- Talk about upcoming vacations and trips.
- Review your marital needs by asking your partner what you can do for them and what they might especially need from you in the coming week.
- Review any intimacy issues that need to be discussed.

Like with our cars, we do not wait until the engine falls out onto the driveway to make a visit to the mechanic. Instead, we address the first signs of squeaky brakes or an air conditioner that's blowing hot air. We pay attention to the gasoline gauge and fill up when the warning light turns on. Just as we maintain the functionality of our vehicles because they will run better, run smoother, and last longer, we need to maintain open communication in marriage by being willing to discuss physical intimacy with our spouse. Indeed, if couples addressed issues before they become big problems, marriages would become happier and more fulfilling as well.

Talking about sexual intimacy is a skill that requires practice and feedback. It is important to ask your spouse questions and learn from your partner. We compiled the following questions from other sex therapists and questions of our own that couples should ask each other often. Such questions could be addressed in a couples meeting, as well as in other informal settings. These questions can be a catalyst for wonderful discussions about intimacy. Consider the following:[6]

1. What is your favorite way to initiate sex, or what is your favorite way for me to initiate sex?
2. What are you particularly enjoying about our sexual relationship?
3. What are three specific things I do that you like the most?
4. What are three things I do that you like the least?
5. Tell me about one of your favorite sexual experiences we have shared together.
6. What would your ideal sexual encounter be like? Share as many details as you can.
7. What time of day do you prefer to have sex?
8. On a scale of zero to ten (zero being not at all and ten being a lot), how important is nonsexual touch and affection to you in our relationship?
9. What kind of affection do you enjoy the most or least?
10. How satisfied are you with the amount of affection in our marriage? (Highly satisfied, moderately satisfied, slightly satisfied, or dissatisfied.)

---

6 Adapted from Laura M. Brotherson, *Knowing HER Intimately: 12 Keys for Creating a Sextraordinary Marriage* (2016), 218–219.

Discuss how to reach a greater level of satisfaction regarding affection in the marriage.
11. Where and how do you like to be touched? How do you want to experience pleasure?
12. What are some things that happen outside the bedroom that make you more interested in being intimate?
13. What are some things that happen outside the bedroom that make you less interested in being intimate?
14. What do you need from me when we have sex?
15. What kind of talking/sounds during sex do you like, if any?
16. What is something you have thought might be fun to try during physical intimacy?
17. What do you tend to think or worry about most when we are being intimate?
18. What do you think are some of our biggest obstacles or challenges when it comes to sex?
19. What were some of your favorite things about our honeymoon?
20. What do you like to do after sex? (i.e., cuddle, shower, etc.)

Of course, not all these questions need to be addressed in one sitting. Take your time, and perhaps each week, or even each month, address one of these questions, and then go to work on it.

In all conversations, remember the principle of *positive reinforcement*; when we reward positive behavior, it is more likely to occur and continue. Therefore, find positive things about your spouse to share in any discussion—particularly when discussing something as sensitive as physical intimacy. In marriage, always look for the good in your spouse, and praise and compliment your spouse frequently and consistently. Elder Dieter F. Uchtdorf taught,

> Because no matter how flat your relationship may be at the present, if you keep adding pebbles of kindness, compassion, listening, sacrifice, understanding, and selflessness, eventually a mighty pyramid will begin to grow.
>
> ... If we look for imperfections in our spouse or irritations in our marriage, we will certainly find them, because everyone has some. On the other hand, if we look for the good, we will surely find it, because everyone has many good qualities too.
>
> Those who save marriages pull out the weeds and water the flowers. They celebrate the small acts of grace that spark

tender feelings of charity. Those who save marriages save future generations.[7]

Being positive, edifying, and complimentary to your spouse will bless your marriage for a lifetime and perhaps even longer. Another strategy Covey suggests in establishing effective communication is to aim for a win-win scenario.[8] Looking for a win-win instead of just a suitable compromise can be a powerful principle in addressing sexual issues. Establishing a win-win scenario in your marriage consists of these steps: first, make your partner aware of the issue instead of avoiding it; second, come to the conversation open and with a willingness to achieve a positive outcome while letting go of the anger you might feel; third, commit to finding a resolution; fourth, listen with purpose and without judgment; and finally, fifth, find a workable solution by brainstorming ideas with your spouse.[9] This method of communication takes time and patience, but it can be effective in achieving a solution that works for you both.

One example of a win-win scenario would be if a wife shares with her husband that she often feels too tired for sex. The wife expresses that she would like to have more energy and be able to enjoy sex more, but currently, she feels tired, worn out, and she does not have any time to herself. She goes on to say that she feels discouraged, worrying she is not enjoying physical intimacy as she once did and is concerned her husband may be taking it personally. The husband listens and hears his wife say that she would like to enjoy sex more, but that she's often fatigued, and her exhaustion is interfering with their sex life.

As the couple communicates about how the wife feels, the husband listens, and instead of responding defensively ("I am doing a lot too!") or judgmentally ("All you do is stay home all day.") or being critical (asking his wife what she can cut out of her routine because she's taking on too many things and doing too much), the couple brainstorms a win-win scenario. The husband explores the option of taking over the children's morning routines and driving the kids to school three days a week, which will allow his wife to sleep in and get the rest she needs. They begin to come up with a win-win scenario that consists of the husband helping with the morning routine in a way that the wife can begin to feel more rested, loved, and relaxed in order to enjoy sex more. The husband

---

7   Dieter F. Uchtdorf, "In Praise of Those Who Save," *Ensign*, May 2016.
8   *See* Covey, *The 7 Habits of Highly Effective People*.
9   *See* Covey, *The 7 Habits of Highly Effective People*.

also expresses that he would like some additional time with the kids where he is in charge, and they do not always need Mom. This is an example of a win-win scenario where a couple is focused on the best outcome for both partners.

Overall, communication about sex helps to express desire, explore fantasies, and learn more about oneself as well as your spouse. Talking about sex allows couples to listen instead of just respond, express empathy regarding a very personal topic, and make the smallest change that will create the biggest differences when it comes to physical intimacy and your overall marital satisfaction. Lastly, if Salt and Peppa can sing their hit song "Let's Talk about Sex" on the radio over thirty years ago and have it still be popular today, we are confident their message of talking about sex is still very much relevant to all married couples.

Question #14:
How often should couples be intimate?

BESIDES THE QUESTION ABOUT WHAT sexual behaviors are appropriate within marriage, the second most commonly asked question in our informal survey pertains to how often newlywed couples can expect to be physically intimate. Apparently, years ago, President Abraham Lincoln was asked, "How long do you think a man's legs should be?" President Lincoln responded, "Long enough to reach the ground." Therefore, if your legs can reach the ground—then you're good! Likewise, if the sexual relationship in your marriage is fulfilling and meets your needs, then you shouldn't have to worry about quotas or what some survey said. Furthermore, what is appropriate and fulfilling for one couple regarding the sexual relationship may not be suitable for another.

Most people would agree that there are many benefits to having sex—aside from the expected outcome of physical, emotional, and spiritual bonding between husband and wife. Physical intimacy increases a person's overall health, including better heart health, a healthier immune system, and an improvement in sleep. Additionally, sex has been found to lower a person's blood pressure, reduce stress, improve self-esteem, and decrease depression and anxiety. Sexual intimacy is not only physically pleasurable, but it also connects husband and wife together when the hormone oxytocin is released during orgasm. Closeness and connection are vital to marital relationships, and having sex strengthens overall intimacy in couples.[1]

Although there are many advantages to having sex, couples differ in how often they engage in sexual activity. There is not an arbitrary magical number or ideal sexual frequency count for couples. Certainly, sexual frequency in marriage

---

1   *See* Kara Mayer Robinson, "10 Surprising Health Benefits of Sex," *WebMD*, Mar. 6, 2022, https://www.webmd.com/sex-relationships/features/sex-and-health.

depends on many variables, such as age, mood, fatigue, differing schedules, physical health, and a host of other reasons. The difficultly arises when husbands and wives experience a difference in sexual desire. Yet, this is to be expected and is common because each person is unique and cannot be expected to desire sex equally. Moreover, sexual desire changes for individuals throughout their lifetime; therefore, how often couples have sex will change too.

Principle

"And now remember . . . ye are free; ye are permitted to act for yourselves; for behold, God hath given unto you a knowledge and he hath made you free."[2] Heavenly Father has given us our agency and the right to make choices for ourselves. Even though a man and a woman are married, both partners continue to have the right to choose to be physically intimate or not and how often that occurs. President Spencer W. Kimball taught that physical intimacy "does not mean that a woman is the servant of her husband. It does not mean that any man has a right to demand sex anytime that he might want it. He should be reasonable and understanding and it should be a general program between the two, so they understand and everybody is happy about it."[3]

As President Kimball has suggested, no husband should ever force, coerce, badger, or guilt his wife into having a sexual relationship. Likewise, women should not engage in similar tactics to get sex from their husbands. Additionally, couples should not withhold sex as a punishment to their partner either. Instead, husbands and wives should be sensitive to each other's sexual needs and desires while also being considerate of each other's moods, schedules, energy levels, and emotional intimacy within the relationship. Even in marriage, self-control and discipline will often need to be exercised to maintain balance and equilibrium. It is also wise to avoid unrealistic expectations when it comes to your sexual relationship. Again, a marriage license does not suggest that one person owes another person physical intimacy whenever they want it. Instead, communicate openly about your desires and respond to one another with kindness, patience, and understanding. Christlike principles of charity, kindness, and respect should be emphasized in the marriage relationship—especially when it comes to sexual intimacy.

Explanation

When it comes to sex, too often we use the phrase "sex drive" instead of "sexual desire." In truth, a drive is a motivational system that pertains to

---

2 Helaman 14:30.
3 *The Teachings of Spencer W. Kimball*, ed. Edward L. Kimball (1982), 312.

life-and-death issues, such as hunger, thirst, sleep, or maintaining an appropriate body temperature. Simply put, you are not going to die if you do not have sex.[4] Moreover, just like some individuals eat more and some eat less than others, sexual intimacy works in the same fashion. There is no one-size-fits-all expectation for sexual frequency.

Even though there is no "normal" when it comes to how often couples are having sex, many people still wonder what the research indicates pertaining to sexual frequency. As a reminder, studies are not necessarily accurate because participants who self-report may do so incorrectly or embellish certain details. Furthermore, comparisons to other couples on any topic can cause stress and contention. A husband or wife should never use research statistics against their partner as a weapon of coercion or to make them feel inadequate, which is why we hesitate to share them here in this book. However, with a quick Google search, you will find research studies that mention sexual frequency, and we want to discuss their potential implications.

As previously mentioned, many factors affect how often people have sex. For example, people who are in a committed relationship have more sex than those who are not; therefore, married people have sex more often than those who are single.[5] Newlyweds also engage in a higher frequency of sexual intimacy than longer-married couples do.[6] Couples where the wife is in the latter stages of pregnancy or right after the birth of a child tend to have sex less often.[7]

Additionally, the *Kinsey Institute* reported that age is a key factor in how often couples have sex. Researchers found that people under thirty years old have sex approximately 112 times a year or about twice a week. Those between the ages of 30–39 have sex 86 times a year or 1–2 times per week. Individuals between the ages of 40–49 have sex 69 times a year, which is a little more than once a week. Finally, those over 50 have sex 52 times a year or once a week. Clearly, as indicated by these findings, the frequency of sex in a relationship

---

4 *See* Emily Nagoski, *Come As You Are: The Surprising New Science that Will Transform Your Sex Life* (2015), 229–233.
5 *See* Jean M. Twenge, "Declines in Sexual Frequency Among American Adults, 1989–2014," *Archives of Sexual Behavior*, 46 (2017): 2389–2401.
6 *See* William H. James, "The Honeymoon Effect on Marital Coitus," *The Journal of Sex Research*, 17, no. 2, (1981): 114–123.
7 *See* Kirsten Von Sydow, "Sexuality During Pregnancy and After Childbirth: A Metacontent Analysis of 59 Studies," *Journal of Psychosomatic Research*, 47, no. 1 (1999): 27–49.

decreases as age increases.[8] Age may be a factor due to lower energy levels, additional health issues, or men may experience an increased difficulty in achieving and maintaining an erection. Interestingly, even though younger couples have sex more often than older couples, older couples often report higher levels of sexual satisfaction.[9]

Several years ago, some Brigham Young University researchers published a study that examined sexual frequency among LDS couples.[10] Here is what they discovered when they asked the question, "How often do you have sex with your partner?"

How Often Do You Have Sex with Your Partner?

Response	Women	Men
Never	4%	3%
Less than once a month	4%	5%
1–3 times a month	15%	16%
Once a week	22%	23%
2–4 times a week	40%	38%
5–7 times a week	13%	12%
More than once a day	2%	3%

From this data set, it appears that 53 percent of women and 50 percent of men are having sex between two to seven times per week, and almost 75 percent of LDS couples have sex at least weekly.

Many people believe that the more sex a couple has, the happier they will be. However, studies have found that couples who have sex more than once a week are no happier with their relationship than those who have sex

---

8   Anna Rahmanan, "Study Reveals Average Amount of Sex People Are Having at Your Age," *Timeout* (Blog), Aug. 28, 2017, https://www.timeout.com/usa/blog/study-reveals-average-amount-of-sex-people-are-having-at-your-age-082817.

9   *See* S. E. Trompeter, R. Bettencourt, & E. Barrett-Connor, "Sexual Activity and Satisfaction in Healthy Community-Dwelling Older Women," *American Journal of Medicine*, 125, no. 1 (Jan. 2021): 37–43, doi: 10.1016/j.amjmed.2011.07.036.

10 As cited by D. M. Busby, J. S. Carroll, & C. Leavitt in *Sexual Wholeness in Marriage: An LDS Perspective on Integrating Sexuality and Spirituality in our Marriages*, 171.

only once a week. Moreover, having sex more than once a week may decrease sexual desire or the enjoyment of sex.[11]

Nonetheless, how often you choose to have sex should be discussed between you and your partner to determine what is satisfying to you both. You do not need to have more sex simply because other people are reporting that they are having more sex than you are. In addition, you do not need to have sex less often if you both prefer to engage in sexual activity more often than other couples do. However, occasionally, we work with married couples who are not sexually active or who rarely have sex. A sexless marriage is concerning because it indicates a lack of connection between partners. In fact, couples in this situation may want to pursue professional help. Likewise, if there is a spouse who seeks to be physically intimate several times a day, for weeks and months on end, this could also signal a significant problem, and once again, it would be wise to contact a professional counselor to work through these issues.

Practical Application

Keep in mind that the "right amount of sex" is what is right for you, your partner, and not anyone else. The goal of marriage is not how often you can have sex but, rather, to be connected both emotionally and physically to each other. We will address differences in sexual desire in another chapter. Nevertheless, below are some guidelines regarding sexual frequency:

1. *Be respectful of each other.* If your spouse does not want to engage in physical intimacy, do not push them. There will be other days and other opportunities. You can still be close. Husbands, treat your wives tenderly. If your wife is not in the mood to be intimate because she has a headache, give her a head rub. Backrubs and foot rubs are also legendary for helping a spouse feel better and desire to be closer.
2. *Identify and focus on your spouse's love language.* Work on speaking your spouse's love language (www.5lovelanguages.com) and strive to meet their needs—and those needs will not always be sexual.
3. *Communicate about your desired sexual frequency.* If you are married to a spouse who does not want to have sex as often as you do, take the time to talk to them and be considerate of their feelings. Listen to their responses and be empathetic. Perhaps scheduling intimacy or getting away on a romantic weekend could help your partner desire sex more.

---

11   *See* G. Lowenstein, T. Krishnamurti, J. Kopsic, & D. McDonald, "Does Increased Sexual Frequency Enhance Happiness?" *Journal of Economic Behavior and Organization*, 116 (2015): 206–218.

4. *Stay in the present and avoid jumping to conclusions.* As you talk through this personal, vulnerable, and possibly difficult conversation around how often you are having sex, remember to stay in the present, and do not jump to the worst-case scenario or assume the future of your intimate life is doomed. Just because you are not on the same page with how often you are having sex as a couple, that does not mean that it will be that way forever or that you will never be satisfied. Maintain hope that the love you have will continue to help you navigate the challenges that may come with your physical relationship.
5. *Contact a professional counselor.* If the problem is over your heads and you are not progressing in this area, find a good marriage counselor that can help you work your way through these challenges. Often, the counselor can help you communicate more effectively regarding your sexual relationship.

Remember, when it comes to sexual frequency, every couple will be different. Do not compare yourself to what you hear in the media or from friends or family members who talk freely about how much sex they are having. Truly, it is not about the quantity of sex for couples, but instead, it is about the quality of your shared sexual experiences together. The most important thing is what works for you—and that you feel closer to each other and more intimately connected through your physical relationship.

Question #15:
Does the Church have an official stance on what sexual acts are appropriate within marriage? Are there guidelines on what couples can "do" and "not" do?

IN OUR INFORMAL SURVEY OF college students regarding sexual intimacy within marriage, one of the most frequently asked questions proposed by our students was, "Now that we are married, what can we do sexually with each other? Are there any restrictions or limitations?" Others have phrased the question differently by asking, "Is there anything we should *not* do?" Some have even wondered if there is a handbook complete with "dos and don'ts" for newly married couples. Even more, several of our more creative students have wondered if the day will ever come when the Church leaders will publish a handbook called *For the Strength of Adults*. We suppose that this pamphlet would be filled with great information on how to file your taxes, how to hold impressive neighborhood block parties, how to raise teenagers, and of course, how to have a healthy sexual relationship with your spouse. For some reason, we do not feel that this pamphlet will be coming anytime soon. Simply put, adults must figure out many of these issues for themselves.

Principle

The Lord will not spell out or dictate every step we must take in our lives. He expects us to follow the Spirit and make our own decisions. Elder Bruce R. McConkie taught, "It is not, never had been, and never will be the design and purpose of the Lord—however much we seek him in prayer—to answer all our problems and concerns without struggle and effort on our part. This mortality is a probationary estate. In it we have our agency."[1] There is no specific policy in the *Church Handbook* about sexual intimacy between husbands and wives. Instead, the Lord has stated, "For behold, it is not meet

---

1   Bruce R. McConkie, "Why the Lord Ordained Prayer," *Ensign*, Jan. 1976, 11.

that I should command in all things; for he that is compelled in all things, the same is a slothful and not a wise servant; wherefore he receiveth no reward."[2]

Church leaders have elected not to provide detailed direction in this sacred and private area because the physically intimate life between husbands and wives is between them and God. Just as with frequency, when it comes to sexual intimacy and sexual preferences, there is no one-size-fits-all answer. The issues here are too delicate, customized, and personal. Instead, each couple must decide what they are comfortable with and what kind of sexual intimacy is within the appropriate bounds for them. It will be unique and different for each couple—no couple is the same, nor will every couple define what is sexually appropriate in the same way.

Explanation

Although there is no official policy regarding appropriate or inappropriate sexual acts between a husband and wife, Church leaders have given direction and counsel to help guide couples in this area. Many years ago, Elder Boyd K. Packer taught,

> Accept this caution. A married couple may be tempted to introduce things into their relationship that are unworthy. Do not, as the scriptures warn, "change the natural use into that which is against nature" (Romans 1:26). If you do, the tempter will drive a wedge between you. If something unworthy has become part of your relationship, don't ever do it again![3]

When it comes to sexual relations in the marriage, a line can be crossed. There are sexual acts that may be considered more lustful, coarse, lewd, selfish, and maybe even perverse, rather than what true lovemaking should be—care, concern, affection, nurturing, softness, and tenderness. If one partner feels a particular sexual act falls into questionable or uncomfortable territory, it is important for couples to address the issue, discuss it, and if necessary, refrain from participating in the practice and choose a different way to express their love physically.

President Spencer W. Kimball also addressed the natural and the unnatural in the context of sexual intimacy. He taught, "If it is unnatural, you just don't do it. That is all, and all the family life should be kept clean

---

2   Doctrine and Covenants 58:26.
3   Boyd K. Packer, "The Fountain of Life," (devotional given at Brigham Young University, Mar. 29, 1992).

and worthy on a very high plane. There are some people who have said that behind the bedroom doors anything goes. That is not true and the Lord would not condone it."[4] Of course, couples will need to determine what is *natural* and what is not. Perhaps the key to President Kimball's statement was the idea that behind bedroom doors, physical intimacy between couples is not a free-for-all. Disciples of Jesus Christ have always been taught to exert self-control, to be prudent (not necessarily prudish), and to live their lives according to the Spirit.

Mark often explains this principle to his students this way: When you water ski, you can stay behind the boat, or you can cut out so far in the wake that you can pass the boat. Couples who are more conservative sexually are those, figuratively speaking, who stay behind the boat. Make no mistake here—skiing behind the boat can be exciting and thrilling. You can attain high speeds, jump the wake, and make some incredible cuts. However, metaphorically, those who ski way outside of the wake or who even try to pass the boat can be likened to those who push the envelope and involve themselves in less common or unusual sexual practices. In our clinical work with couples, those who engage in these types of sexual practices, especially if one spouse is not in favor of such practices—but their partner pushes them—often develop resentment and even anger in their relationship. Most often, abnormal sexual practices are no longer driven by love and mutual care and respect for each other, but by selfishness, lust, and carnality.

Including the Lord in your marriage and counseling together as a couple helps husbands and wives identify what is sexually appropriate for their marital relationship. Couples should seek to stay on the Lord's side of the line and to seek the guidance of the Spirit pertaining to their sexual lives. The Holy Ghost is our constant companion. Believe it or not, if we are worthy, that Spirit will be with us even during times of intimacy with our spouse. As couples engage in sexual practices that are uncomfortable, feel forced, or disregard a partner's feelings altogether, the Holy Ghost may withdraw—and couples will immediately feel the loss of the Spirit.

The word *intimacy* means closeness, connection, and familiarity. President Howard W. Hunter provided a key concept regarding intimacy when he taught, "Each partner must be considerate and sensitive to the other's needs and desires. Any domineering, indecent, or uncontrolled behavior in the intimate relationship between husband and wife is condemned by the Lord."[5]

---

4   *The Teachings of Spencer W. Kimball*, ed. Edward L. Kimball (1982), 312.
5   Howard W. Hunter, "Being a Righteous Husband and Father," *Ensign*, Nov. 1994, 51.

Physical intimacy is designed to strengthen the bond between husbands and wives and increase unity between partners. Author Laura Brotherson, who specializes in couples therapy and sexual issues, wrote,

> What's the point of someone even saying that a particular behavior is okay, if your spouse feels that it isn't? The counsel would only be useful for the one spouse to, in essence, beat the other spouse over the head about it. That's not the best way to create a close and intimate loving relationship. This is why couples must take responsibility for working through their intimate differences between themselves and God, if needed, based on divine principles.[6]

In addition, intimacy includes privacy. What occurs sexually between couples is private and special. It should be discussed between partners and not shared with others outside the relationship except for an intention to seek help, ask questions, or gather additional information. Couples should be able to trust each other that their sex life will not be described in detail to garner attention or to gather material for a stand-up comedy routine. Trust increases for couples who maintain each other's privacy in the bedroom.

Perhaps the question "What can we do sexually in our marriage?" is the wrong question to be asking. Perhaps individuals should be more focused on expressing their love to their spouse and asking each other how they can better meet their needs. President Gordon B. Hinckley advised, "I am satisfied that a happy marriage is not so much a matter of romance as it is an anxious concern for the comfort and well-being of one's companion. . . . Selfishness is the antithesis of love."[7] When selfishness becomes the driving factor in a sexual relationship, then lust, rather than love, is manifested. When a spouse becomes egocentric or self-absorbed regarding their sexual life, the husband-wife relationship can become compromised or even damaged.

Charity, respect, kindness, compassion, empathy, and love are the guiding principles in the intimate relationship. Dr. Linda Wait and Dr. Maggie Gallagher have stated that selfless sexual relations can "literally double your sexual pleasure: you get satisfaction not only from your own sexual response but from your partner's as well . . . love and concern for one's partner shifts the

---

6 Laura M. Brotherson, *Knowing HER Intimately: 12 Keys for Creating a Sextraordinary Marriage* (2016), 36.
7 Gordon B. Hinckley, "What God Hath Joined Together," *Ensign*, May 1991, 73.

focus away from the self in a sexual relationship and toward the other person. This selfless approach to sex, paradoxically, is far more likely to bring sexual satisfaction to both men and women."[8] Thus, it is important to remember that specific sexual acts do not create the intimacy that is desired as much as listening to and honoring your partner's body and feelings does.

Practical Application

Ultimately, respect is at the core of healthy marital relationships. Therefore, it is vital to show respect to your partner in the bedroom, and any sexual act that feels disrespectful to your spouse ought to be avoided. No spouse should be placed in a position where they feel demeaned, objectified, degraded, or used by their partner. Moreover, a spouse should never feel that during sex, they have lost their dignity or even their identity.

Couples can demonstrate respect when they have open and candid conversations, especially after their wedding, regarding what they feel is sexually appropriate and mutually enjoyable. As has been mentioned before, couples should discuss with each other their sexual desires, likes and dislikes, and what they are comfortable with in the bedroom. Specifically, topics of discussion may include sexual positions, locations for sex, specific sexual acts, and a host of other practices.

Brigham Young University Professors Dean Busby, Jason Carroll, and Chelom Leavitt suggested that when couples make decisions regarding their sexual behaviors, they should carefully consider the following four questions:

1. Does this particular behavior strengthen our relationship with each other and with God?
2. Do we both agree about this aspect of our sexuality?
3. Does this reflect a positive and healthy attitude about sexuality?
4. Does this nurture the sexual needs of my spouse and myself?[9]

Keep in mind that "these questions should not be answered by simply labeling certain behaviors as 'right' or 'wrong'; rather, you should thoughtfully consider the motives and consequences of proposed sexual behaviors."[10]

---

8   L. Waite & M. Gallagher, *The Case for Marriage* (2000), 89; *see also* D. M. Busby, J. S. Carroll, & C. Leavitt, *Sexual Wholeness in Marriage: An LDS Perspective on Integrating Sexuality and Spirituality in Our Marriages* (2013), 152.
9   D. M. Busby, J. S. Carroll, & C. Leavitt, *Sexual Wholeness in Marriage: An LDS Perspective on Integrating Sexuality and Spirituality in Our Marriages*, 118–119.
10 Busby, Carroll, Leavitt, *Sexual Wholeness in Marriage*, 119.

Kevin A. Thompson, a Christian pastor who often speaks on the topic of marriage, wrote, "Few people understand the connection between respect and good sex. Yet the two are greatly related. When respect is present in a relationship, husband[s] and wives will value one another. They will learn how to give and receive pleasure. They will be able to communicate in a way that overcomes problems and teaches each other how to be better lovers."[11] As couples strive for and seek to understand what will strengthen and bind them closer together, they will be able to resolve differing opinions and preferences in their intimate relationship and create a solid foundation of trust and connection that will bless them throughout their marriage.

---

11   Kevin A. Thompson, "The Only Thing That's Off Limits in Bed," *Kevin A. Thompson* (blog), https://www.kevinathompson.com/off-limits-bed/.

Question #16:
If sexual problems are one of the leading causes of divorce, what are some common marital intimacy problems?

OVER THE YEARS, MANY HEADLINES and pundits have touted that sexual problems are the number-one cause of divorce. To give you some peace of mind, that is not true. Today, the number one reason for divorce is a lack of commitment. In fact, in a recent national study,[1] 73 percent of the respondents reported that a lack of commitment was their reason for divorce, followed by too much arguing (56 percent), infidelity (55 percent), marrying too young (46 percent), unrealistic expectations (45 percent), lack of equality in the relationship (44 percent), lack of preparation for marriage (41 percent), and abuse (29 percent).[2] In another study, 55 percent of the respondents said that growing apart was the number-one reason for their divorce; 53 percent attributed "not able to talk together" as the cause of their break-up; and 24 percent reported that sexual problems were an important reason for the dissolution of their marriage.[3]

Therefore, the historical reasons for divorce—money and sex—do not seem to be the leading causes any longer. Granted, sexual problems could be embedded in "lack of commitment," or "too much arguing," or "infidelity" for sure, but sexual problems are not the prime reasons why marriages break up—they are most likely a symptom of the problem. Do sexual problems weaken marriages and cause unhappiness and dissatisfaction in contemporary relationships? Absolutely! Therefore, couples should prepare themselves to deal with potential sexual challenges in their marriage.

---

1 In this study, participants could vote for multiple answers, so the percentages do not add up to 100.
2 See "With This Ring: A National Survey on Marriage in America," *The National Fatherhood Initiative*, 2005, https://www.fatherhood.org/with-this-ring-survey.
3 See A. J. Hawkins, B. J. Willoughby, & W. J. Doherty, "Reasons for divorce and openness to marital reconciliation," *Journal of Divorce and Remarriage* 53, no. 6 (2012): 453–463.

Although we have recommended that couples *should not* build their marriage on the foundation of sex, sexual relations in marriage can serve as a barometer of the quality of the marital relationship. Dr. Jan Parker, a licensed marriage and family therapist with more than twenty years in private practice and thirty years in education teaching human sexuality, writes, "I've worked with a lot of individuals and couples who are having trouble in their relationship and that's leading to difficulties sexually because sex is one of those places that relationship issues show up fairly quickly. When people don't feel connected, or safe or loved or cared about, then sex either goes away or becomes fairly mechanical."[4] Thus, sexual problems can be a mask for actual relational issues.

Principle

"For it must needs be, that there is an opposition in all things."[5] Opposition in *all* things includes, well, everything! Each of us will encounter opposition in our personal life, professional life, Church life, family life, marriage life, and yes, even in our intimate sexual lives with our partner. No one can escape opposition—especially in a marriage setting. Just as in other aspects of your life, opposition can build strength, and it's an opportunity for growth. In fact, a couple's ability to bounce back from adversity increases a couple's resiliency. Researchers have found that people who face a moderate level of adversity in their lives experience better mental health and report a higher level of satisfaction with their lives compared to those who do not experience hardships.[6]

In addition, adversity tends to increase a person's empathy for others, build self-confidence, help a person appreciate the good in life, and provide spiritual development.[7] Elder Dieter F. Uchtdorf said, "It is your reaction to adversity, not the adversity itself, that determines how your life's story will develop."[8] Difficulties in marriage become an opportunity for a husband and wife to

---

4   Jan Parker, "Getting Clinical Skills in Human Sexuality Psychology," *National University*, https://www.nu.edu/resources/getting-clinical-skills-in-human-sexuality-psychology/.
5   2 Nephi 2:11.
6   *See* Mark D. Seery, E. Alison Holman, & Roxane Cohen Silver, "Whatever Does Not Kill Us: Cumulative Lifetime Adversity, Vulnerability, and Resilience," *Journal of Personality and Social Psychology* 99, no. 6 (2010): 1025–1041.
7   *See* Paula Davis, "How Adversity Makes You Stronger," *Forbes Online Magazine* (Mar. 26, 2020), https://www.forbes.com/sites/pauladavislaack/2020/03/26/adversity-makes-you-stronger/?sh=72d8384b5709.
8   Dieter F. Uchtdorf, "Your Happily Ever After," *Ensign* or *Liahona*, May 2010.

come together and overcome the challenges they face. Not all couples do it successfully; but for those who do, they can experience an even closer and more meaningful relationship.

Explanation
Our coauthor, Doug, and Dr. Stephen Lamb reported that about 30 percent of men and 40 percent of women experience sexual problems at any given time.[9] From our own professional experiences, it appears that some of the most common sexual problems that couples encounter include the following:
1. Low libido or sexual desire
2. Sexual expectation differences
3. Desire discrepancy—one partner wants to have sex when the other does not
4. Lack of other types of intimacy (emotional, intellectual, experiential, spiritual)
5. Boredom with sex life
6. Difficulty becoming sexually aroused
7. Painful intercourse
8. Inability to find sexual fulfillment
9. High or unrealistic expectations regarding sexual frequency
10. Sex is a low priority due to busy schedules or not enough time for each other
11. Media, television in bedroom, social media, too much time on cell phones/electronics
12. Low satisfaction with body image
13. Stress and/or fatigue
14. Children (pregnancy, nursing, infertility, parenting, etc.)
15. Depression, anxiety, or other mental health issues
16. Pornography and sexual addictions
17. Previous sexual abuse or trauma
18. Infidelity
19. Medications that reduce sexual desire
20. Performance anxiety
21. Erectile dysfunction

Knowing about these potential problems will help you navigate your way through them more productively. We also address several of these topics specifically in other chapters of this book.

---
9 Uchtdorf, "Your Happily Ever After."

Practical Application

One of the great myths of our day is that disagreements, quarrels, and contention only occur in bad marriages. This is simply not true! Conflict, to some degree, exists in all marriages. Of course, sexual differences and difficulties are universal issues couples will encounter that can produce potential conflict. The issue is not whether conflict exists, but how a couple manages the conflicts that they experience. Establishing healthy communication skills is essential to resolving conflict within marriage, no matter what the topic is.

Psychologist John Gottman has spent his career studying couples' communication patterns. He and his research team observed husbands and wives discussing challenging issues within their marriage. They were able to predict with over 90 percent accuracy whether a couple would stay together based on the way a couple communicated. Results from Gottman's research indicated that there are four types of communication that negatively impact marital relationships. Gottman identified them as criticism, contempt, defensiveness, and stonewalling, calling them "The 4 Horsemen of the Apocalypse."[10]

Criticism is the first horseman and is defined as an attack on your partner's character. Dr. Gottman and his team define criticism very differently than a complaint. A complaint is an expression of dissatisfaction with a particular situation. To combat this "horseman," it's imperative to use "I" statements and express your feelings and needs clearly. For example, a wife may say, "I feel lonely and disappointed when you stay after work and do not tell me that you aren't coming home on time. I need you to text me if you're staying late and what time you think you might be home."

Conversely, criticism includes judging your partner based on their faults. Following the illustration above, an example of this wife's criticism would be, "You never tell me when you are coming home from work. That is so selfish, and you are only thinking about yourself." Being critical of your spouse deteriorates the relationship and opens the door to the other horsemen to be present in your marriage as well. When couples use and place emphasis on "I" to voice their complaints instead of "you," it allows for expression of feelings instead of blame. Dr. Gottman suggests that "I" statements contribute to a soft start-up to the conversation between husband and wife and can enhance communication about difficult issues.

Contempt is the second horseman and is the single greatest predictor of divorce. Contempt is criticism turned nasty. It occurs when you treat your

---

10   John Gottman, *Why Marriages Succeed or Fail* (1995).

spouse with disdain, often making them feel worthless. It includes ridiculing, mocking, name-calling, mimicking, and even eye-rolling. It goes beyond being critical and instead comes from a position of superiority. One example would be, "I've been at work all day and what have you done? Laid on the couch watching your shows? The house is a mess, the kids still have their pajamas on, and we don't even have any groceries for dinner. You're so lazy!" When you insult and belittle your partner, it is extremely destructive to your marriage. If this is happening in your communication with your partner in any way, it's imperative that it stops. To counteract this "horseman," learn how to communicate more effectively without harming your spouse, and focus on the positive attributes of your spouse, finding gratitude for what he or she brings to the marriage.

Defensiveness is the third horseman, and it typically occurs when a person feels attacked. By nature, we tend to defend ourselves; however, this approach is a sign that a person isn't listening to their partner, and they are refusing to take responsibility for their actions. An example of defensiveness would be the following:

Wife: "Why didn't you tell me you would be late?"

Husband: "It's not my fault that I didn't have time to call you. There was traffic on the way home, and my boss needed me to finish something!"

Instead, a non-defensive response accepts responsibility for the feelings of your partner, admits fault, and apologizes. This demonstrates an ability to listen and express empathy. Thus, a more effective response from the husband would be, "I'm sorry. I should have taken a moment to let you know I would be late. My boss wanted me to finish a project at work, but I realize that I put you in a bind by arriving home later than expected. I will make sure to communicate that in the future." Even though the situation may not be directly that person's fault, their actions have still led to unpleasant feelings or inconveniences for their spouse. To combat this horseman, acknowledge your mistakes, own your faults, and apologize for them instead of defending yourself and making excuses.

Stonewalling is the fourth and final horseman, and it includes shutting down, withdrawing, and simply not talking to your spouse. It is the scariest horseman of all because there isn't just poor communication—there isn't any communication at all. Instead of conflict, there's avoidance, tuning out your partner, being overly busy, using distractions, and not engaging. It's okay to take a time-out when you are overwhelmed or when an attempt at conflict resolution is not going well. However, the key is to come back together to discuss the issue and not avoid it altogether. To counter this "horseman," couples need to learn how to self-soothe when they choose to take the time-out: go for a walk, reach out to a friend, take a shower, listen to music, engage in a favorite hobby, or anything that allows the person to calm down and think about how to manage the conversation differently than before. Then, it is important to reapproach each other and continue the conversation, because when a couple stops talking, it could be a sign of the beginning of the end.

As with discovering what kinds of communication patterns negatively affect a marital relationship, Gottman has also identified ways for couples to increase connection and experience healthier communication. Helpful communication skills during conflict include listening to your partner and reflecting back what your partner is saying to make sure you are hearing them correctly, making eye contact and paying attention to your partner, being aware of your body language as you discuss difficult topics, asking your partner to share more and say more, validating you partner's feelings, expressing empathy, taking responsibility if you've hurt your partner, and showing affection with touch.

Furthermore, according to Gottman, couples have emotional bank accounts that are especially worth the investment. Building up positive experiences during the small, daily interactions of life helps couples to stay connected and thrive despite the conflict they may encounter. In fact, research shows that it takes five positive interactions to balance out one negative interaction.[11] So, it is imperative to focus on creating the good moments so that when the bad ones come, they do not hit nearly as hard.

One way for a couple to make more deposits in their emotional bank account is for couples to build their love maps or get to know their partner.[12] And if you think you know your partner well, come to know them even better. Knowing your partner's likes and dislikes, their values, fears, hopes, and dreams will help you better understand each other.[13] It is vital to ask your partner questions, to remember the answers, and to continue to ask them questions over time.[14] Knowing and truly understanding one another helps reduce negative patterns of communication when problems in the relationship arise.

Additionally, when couples love and respect each other, they are more likely able to withstand the challenges and difficulties they may face. We

---

11   *See* John Gottman, *Seven Principles for Making Marriage Work* (2015).
12   *See* Gottman, *Seven Principles for Making Marriage Work*.
13   *See* Gottman, *Seven Principles for Making Marriage Work*.
14   *See* Kyle Benson, "Three Steps to Reconnect When You Feel Disconnected from Your Partner," *The Gottman Institute*, https://www.gottman.com/blog/3-steps-reconnect-feel-disconnected-partner/.

recommend that instead of focusing on a partner's faults, that we recognize their positive attributes and the good that they do. Expressing kindness and appreciation will strengthen the marriage and the bond between husbands and wives. Furthermore, it's important to directly articulate what you admire about your partner so that they hear it and feel connected to you, knowing you appreciate them and that they matter. Appreciating and respecting one another more helps couples communicate about the challenges they may encounter in a more productive and less harmful manner.

Finally, Gottman insists that as couples turn toward each other, instead of away from each other, they will foster connection and strengthen trust and security in the relationship. Couples bid for each other's attention daily, and as they reach out to each other, it's important to show up and meet the needs of our partners, no matter how small they may be.[15] Gottman has stated, "Couples often ignore each other's emotional needs out of mindlessness, not malice."[16] So, respond to her text, pick up something at the grocery store he needs, unload the dishwasher when you see the "clean" light turn on, give the kids a bath even though your partner usually does it, hand your partner the sunscreen as they step outside in the blinding sun to attend a kid's soccer game, and call each other just to say, "Hello," even though you'll be home in ten minutes. Finding ways to turn toward each other is as simple as acknowledging one another, and it helps fortify your union when trouble arises.

Elder Bruce C. Hafen wrote, "The difference between a successful and an unsuccessful marriage is not in whether there are such times of tension, but in whether and how the tensions are resolved."[17] So, the issue is not *if* you will have challenges or not (sexual or otherwise) but *how* you will solve those challenges together.

Therapists and researchers agree that "*genuine* sexual intimacy has a remarkable power to heal, renew, refresh, restore, and sustain the marriage relationship."[18] Marriage expert Michele Weiner Davis explained, "Sex is an extremely important part of marriage. When it's good, it offers couples opportunities to give and receive physical pleasure, to connect emotionally and

---

15   Benson, "Three Steps to Reconnect."
16   Patricia Morgan, "Book Summary: The Seven Principles for Making a Marriage Work," Solutions for Resilience, accessed 1 Oct. 2023.
17   Bruce C. Hafen, *The Broken Heart* (1989), 49.
18   E. Wheat & G. Wheat, *Intended for Pleasure*, 4th ed. (2022), 135.

spiritually. It builds closeness, intimacy, and a sense of partnership. It defines their relationship as different from all others. Sex is a powerful tie that binds."[19]

Therefore, when it comes to sexual issues within a relationship, couples will need to recognize and address them using healthy communication patterns and avoiding criticism, contempt, defensiveness, and stonewalling. They must build their love map, express their appreciation and respect, and turn toward each other in their daily interactions. This will help to ensure that physical intimacy can be the renewing, bonding, and fulfilling experience couples long for it to be.

---

19   Michele Weiner Davis, *The Sex-Starved Marriage* (2004), 8.

Question #17:
What do you do when you want to have sex and your spouse does not?

As we discussed in a previous chapter, our Father in Heaven created each of His children differently, and because we are all individuals with different desires and needs, a husband's and wife's desires for intimacy will not always coincide. Mark shared the following experience: A recently young married student came to his office after having been married for less than a year. After some small talk, the student said, "Could I ask you a very personal question?" Mark replied that he was game that day for any question. The student then asked, "I just don't know what to do. Usually, when I desire to have sex, my wife has no interest, and when she is in the mood for sex, I am usually too tired or exhausted. Is this normal?" Mark assured his young married student that this tendency was very common, and that this phenomenon was something that practically every married couple experiences. In the real world, and in real time, most couples do not necessarily desire intimacy simultaneously. Even so, men and women are different—different in temperament, different in chemical constitution, different emotionally, different in how we communicate, different in backgrounds, different in life experiences, and certainly different sexually.

Busby and colleagues explained,

> Perhaps the most common sexual difference between spouses is in the desired frequency of sexual intimacy. It is very common for one spouse to have a noticeably stronger desire for sexual stimulation than their spouse. This influences expectations for how often couples will have sex. Research shows that husbands

typically desire sex more frequently than their wives; sometimes this pattern is reversed, with the wife having the higher desire.[1]

Sexual Desire Discrepancy (SDD) is the difference between one's desired frequency of sexual intercourse and the actual frequency of sexual intercourse within a relationship. In 2011, researchers found that 42 percent of women and 54 percent of men were dissatisfied with how often they were having sex with their partner. In addition, the men and women who were unhappy with the sexual frequency in their relationship were more likely to report a decrease in their overall relationship satisfaction as well.[2] Therefore, it is possible that almost half the people in committed sexual relationships right now are unsatisfied with their sexual frequency, and it is affecting their relationships in a negative way.

Even more, SDD is the number-one cause of sexual dysfunction within marriage. SDD can increase conflict among partners as well as the overall instability within the relationship.[3] Consequently, there will be occasions in your marriage when you and your partner will be satisfied with the amount of sex you are having and times when a husband or wife is not particularly interested in sex as much as their spouse is. Considering that this tendency is normal and natural for all couples to experience, it is important to explore the different types of sexual desire a person may experience as well as how couples can increase sexual desire and decrease the barriers that prevent a person from wanting sex more often.

Principle

The Apostle Paul taught, "Let the husband render unto the wife due benevolence: and likewise also the wife unto the husband."[4] The Greek word for "benevolence" (*eunoia*) suggests good will or kindness. Other synonyms

---

1 D. M. Busby, J. S. Carroll, & C. Leavitt, *Sexual Wholeness in Marriage: An LDS Perspective on Integrating Sexuality and Spirituality in Our Marriages* (2013), 103–104.
2 *See* Anthony Smith, Anthony Lyons, Jason Ferris, Juliet Richters, Marian Pitts, Julia Shelly, and Judy M. Simpson, "Sexual and Relationship Satisfaction Among Heterosexual Men and Women: The Importance of Desired Frequency of Sex," *Journal of Sex & Marital Therapy*, 37, no. 2 (March 2011): 104–115, https://doi: 10.1080/0092623X.2011.560531.
3 *See* Brian J. Willoughby and Jennifer Vitas, "Sexual Desire Discrepancy: The Effect of Individual Differences in Desired and Actual Sexual Frequency on Dating Couples," *Archives of Sexual Behavior* 41 (May 2011): 477–486, https://doi.org/10.1007/s10508-011-9766-9.
4 1 Corinthians 7:3.

for "benevolence" include generosity, a desire or disposition to do good, compassion, empathy, love, and charity. There is no more practical institution to practice benevolence and Christlike love than in a marriage. Simply put, to show a spouse benevolence is to be in tune to their needs, show them love, and exercise compassion. It is to treat them how they wish to be treated.[5] President David O. McKay taught, "Benevolence in its fullest sense is the sum of moral excellence and comprehends every other virtue. It is the motive that prompts us to do good to others and leads us to live our life for Christ's sake. All acts of kindness, of self-denial, of self-devotion, of forgiveness, of charity, of love, spring from this divine attribute."[6]

Practicing benevolence within marriage does not require that you have sex any time your partner requests it. It takes both partners to communicate, compromise, exercise patience, and make efforts in satisfying each other's sexual desires. When one partner in a marriage wants to have sex and the other spouse does not, it is important to be compassionate and show empathy. Be careful not to make the person who wants sex feel weird or the person who is not in the mood to have sex feel like something is wrong with him or her. During these times specifically, you will need to work together to understand each other's perspectives and feelings.

In *A Parent's Guide*, it states that

> both husbands and wives have physical, emotional, psychological, and spiritual needs associated with this sacred act . . . Couples will discover differences in the needs or desires each partner has for such a relationship, but when each strives to satisfy the needs of the other, these differences need not present a serious problem. Remember, this intimate relationship between husband and wife was established to bring joy to them. An effort to reach this righteous objective will enable married couples to use their complementary natures to bring joy to this union.[7]

Joy comes from listening to your partner, understanding their emotional and physical desires, and working together to maintain a deep connection

---

5 *See* Matthew 7:12.
6 David O. McKay, "Christ, the Light of Humanity," *Improvement Era*, June 1968, 4.
7 *A Parent's Guide* (1985), 47; *see also* Laura Brotherson, *And They Were Not Ashamed: Strengthening Marriage Through Sexual Fulfillment* (2014), 83–106.

through intimacy. Once again, it is not about your sexual frequency, but instead, it is about seeking satisfaction for both partners without guilt or shame but rather with love and compassion.

Explanation

To explore sexual desire, it is important to note that sexual desire and sexual arousal are two different and distinct constructs. Researchers formerly believed sexual desire preceded sexual arousal, but researchers now understand these constructs are more interconnected, and you can have one without the other.[8] Typically, arousal indicates a physical response in the body. However, renowned sex educator and researcher Emily Nagoski writes that physical arousal does not indicate desire, but instead, if you want to know if your partner is aroused, "you must listen to your partner's *words*, not their genitals."[9] Simply because a man wakes up in the morning with an erection does not mean he is ready and wanting to have sex. Likewise, if a woman experiences vaginal wetness, it does not imply that she desires to have sex right then and there. Thus, a genital response does not equal desire, but instead, sexual desire happens in the brain.

Sexual desire can be categorized as either spontaneous or responsive. Spontaneous desire is when the desire to have sex happens instantaneously and without stimulation. It happens in 75 percent of men and 15 percent of women. In contrast, responsive desire materializes in response to stimulation and occurs in 5 percent of men and 30 percent of women. The remaining 50 percent of women and 20 percent of men also experience responsive desire, but it is specifically context-dependent, or it depends on the circumstances.[10] As Emily Nogoski puts it, "desire comes along when arousal meets a great context."[11] Both spontaneous and responsive desires are completely normal and exist in healthy sexual relationships. Simply because someone has more of a responsive sexual desire rather than a spontaneous one does not mean something is wrong with them or they have a lower sexual desire than their partner. It just means they have different styles of sexual desire altogether.

---

8 *See* Kristen Mark, Debby Herbenick, Dennis Fortenberry, Stephanie Sanders, and Michael Reese, "The Object of Sexual Desire: Examining the 'What' in 'What Do You Desire,'" *Journal of Sexual Medicine* 11, no. 11 (2014): 2709.
9 Emily Nagoski, *Come as You Are: The Surprising New Science That Will Transform Your Sex Life* (2021), 193.
10 *See* Nagoski, *Come As You Are*.
11 Nagoski, *Come As You Are*, 226.

In setting up the appropriate context or the right circumstances for sex, Nagoski writes that it is important to "[turn] on the ons and [turn] off the offs."[12] The turns-ons refer to what accelerates your sexual response, or the "accelerators," and the turn-offs refer to the inhibitors to your sexual response, or the "brakes." Desire occurs by activating the accelerator and deactivating the brakes, and it is affected by how sensitive you are to stimulation. Nonetheless, a sensitive brake is the ultimate predictor of sexual problems despite the accelerator. Therefore, a person may be aroused and there may be sexual stimuli in their environment (anything you see, touch, smell, hear, taste, or envision that your brain has learned to correlate with sexual arousal), but if too many factors are inhibiting that person and pressing on the brake, he or she still will not want to have sex.[13]

For example, let's say a woman thinks she would like to have sex, and her husband washed the dishes and bathed the kids that night. She still could not want sex based on her child crying in his crib as he tries to fall asleep. No matter what looks good and feels good to her, when her children are crying or upset, that automatically hits the brakes and stops any sexual desire she could have experienced. Another example may be when a man enjoys a day with his family, goes to church, and sex sounds pretty good to him as he imagines alone time with his wife in the evening. However, the stress of Monday coming and a rapidly approaching work deadline, along with an impatient boss, causes enough stress to hit the brakes hard enough that the sexual desire never manifests.

As far as the differences between men and women, in a stereotypical sense, men tend to have a more sensitive accelerator and women tend to have a more sensitive brake. Thus, men are more easily turned on, whereas women are more easily turned off. Note that we did not say that women are difficult to turn on or that women have a lower sexual desire. The research merely shows that to heighten arousal, it is important to increase sexually relevant stimuli and decrease what inhibits it.[14]

Practical Application

Overall, improving the context for sexual desire is the key to increasing your sexual satisfaction. Context includes what is happening in the present moment. It includes your partner and your attraction to him or her as well as

---

12 Nagoski, *Come As You Are*, 61.
13 *See* Nagoski, *Come As You Are*.
14 *See* Nagoski, *Come As You Are*.

the level of emotional intimacy you share, the setting of where you and your partner are, the situation you are both in, and the state of mind you both have currently. We suggest you make your own list of turn-ons and turn-offs and discuss with your partner how to improve the context for sexual desire within your marriage. We have made some suggestions of topics listed below to consider and explore together.

Turn-Ons/Turn-Offs

1. **Physical appearance.** A turn-on as it pertains to physical appearance may be a certain outfit your partner is wearing, like that amazing red dress or that certain blue shirt that brings out the color of your partner's eyes. In contrast, it can be a turn-off when your partner does not keep up with their physical appearance or does not seem to care much about it.
2. **Hygiene.** Hygiene includes how you take care of your physical body (i.e., washing your body and your hair, brushing your teeth, wearing deodorant, and putting on clean clothes). A turn-on may be a certain type of smell to your partner's shampoo, body spray, or perfume/cologne. A turn-off can be his or her bad breath, or body odor from exercise, or a general lack of personal hygiene.
3. **Physical exercise.** Activity that raises your heart rate can excite you, and your brain attributes that excitement to the person you are with.[15] Some examples may be taking a bike ride together, hiking together, or simply going on a walk around the neighborhood together. If your heart rate goes up, so does your sexual desire.
4. **Self-confidence.** Confidence is a turn-on because people are drawn to others who like who they are and believe they have something to offer in a relationship. It is attractive to experience that positive, confident energy, and it can increase sexual desire for your partner. Conversely, low self-confidence can inhibit sexual desire by preventing a person from initiating sex or responding to sexual advances.
5. **Set the mood.** By focusing on the human body's five senses, you can increase sexual desire. Visual turn-ons may include lingerie, a certain hairstyle, or seeing your partner play with the kids. Audio turn-ons may include romantic music, peace and quiet, or verbal affirmations from your partner. Taste may include eating dessert together, chewing mint-flavored gum to freshen one's breath, or having hot chocolate together.

---

15   *See* Nagoski, *Come As You Are*, 246.

Smell may include a particular perfume/cologne, lighting a scented candle, or spraying essential oils on your bedsheets. Finally, touch may include hugging or kissing, a certain texture of blankets, silk sheets, that special place you like to be touched, or any kind of affection that feels good. Turn-offs regarding mood-setting may include distractions like loud noises, children crying, an uncomfortable bed, bright lights, tasting your partner's onions from lunch when you kiss, or smelling the litter box from the corner of the room.

6. **Quality of your relationship.** Turn-ons include experiences that build trust and emotional bonding between partners. Sharing your thoughts and feelings, talking about your day, strengthening your friendship, and parenting together can help a couple feel closer to each other. Turn-offs happen when a partner breaks trust or pulls away emotionally from his or her partner. If you want to increase sexual desire and intimacy, improve your closeness and connection.

7. **Feeling desired.** It is a turn-on to feel like your partner is attracted to you. When your partner notices you, pays attention to you, flirts with you, and communicates that desire nonverbally as well as verbally, it helps to increase sexual desire. A turn-off would be to feel ignored, dismissed, or insignificant to your partner.

8. **Setting.** The setting of sexual desire is important. Some couples like to have privacy while others are completely responsive to having sex in more adventurous places. A turn-on might be on the balcony of your hotel room overlooking the beach and a turn-off might be having sex at your mother-in-law's house. Discuss your favorite places or times of the day where you feel like the context is right for sex.

9. **Special occasions.** Special occasions such as anniversaries, birthdays, Valentine's Day, or vacations can be times to focus on increasing sexual desire. Talk about what plans you have, set the scene for romance, be adventurous, and create new sexual experiences. A turn-off would be expecting sex on these days and not being empathetic toward your partner if what you envision doesn't work out. Be flexible and remember it is a time for connection, not expectation.

10. **Specific sexual acts.** Discuss what you like and what you don't like about sex that may affect your desire, such as certain sexual positions, types of foreplay, the use of sex toys, or varying aspects of sexual intercourse. If most people experience responsive desire, then it is important to ask each other, "What do you respond to the most physically?" Remember

that this can change throughout the years, so a couple should continue to assess this topic. In addition, it is important to keep in mind that you will want more sex with your partner if it is the kind of sex you like.

11. **Schedule a time for sex.** You can schedule a day and time during the week to have sex, which might help both partners prepare and make room for sexual desire to be initiated. Although "planning" for sex seems counterintuitive, many couples in our private practices have commented that this proactive approach has helped them prioritize their sexual relationship and has, consequently, strengthened their marriages.

Overall, having a different sexual desire type from your partner is normal, and now that you understand how it contributes to sexual desire discrepancy, you can be more compassionate and less critical of your partner. Having different levels of sexual desire between partners is not what contributes to problems within a marriage specifically, but rather, it is how a couple handles those differences that matters. Learn to express your feelings about your own sexual desire, your accelerators as well as your brakes, and work together to compromise and understand each other. Finally, instead of focusing on the frequency of sex, it is more important to focus on the context in which sexual desire can happen.

Question #18:
Is it selfish to tell your spouse no to sex?

SAYING NO TO A SEXUAL relationship with your spouse can be challenging, especially when it comes to making that statement to the love of your life. However, everyone has limits, and saying no itself is not selfish; in fact, it can actually be healthy. If we do not say no and set boundaries with others, including our spouse, we run the risk of increasing stress, anxiety, depression, and resentment within our relationships. Therefore, setting boundaries helps to clarify expectations and reinforce self-care.

When it comes to having sex or engaging in specific sexual activity within marriage, learning to say no is more appropriate than trying to change your spouse's sexual desire or shaming your partner for wanting sex in the first place. Let us be clear—wanting sex is not the problem, but instead, it is the lack of setting boundaries that can cause issues regarding physical intimacy. Often, a husband or wife will choose to engage in more sexual activity or sexual acts than they desire and then resent their spouse because he or she did not stop them from doing so. Problems arise when we blame someone else for our own lack of establishing limits.

Boundaries should first be communicated with your spouse verbally and then followed up with action. Dr. Cloud and Dr. Townsend, authors of a book entitled *Boundaries*, write, "An important thing to remember about boundaries is that they exist, and they will affect us, whether or not we communicate them."[1] Setting limits includes being direct, open, and transparent with your partner regarding physical intimacy. If we do not communicate our limits directly, then they will be communicated indirectly or nonverbally in other ways, such as through withdrawal, pouting, triangulation (divulging details

---

1   Henry Cloud and Dr. John Townsend, *Boundaries* (2017), 103.

to our friends or family instead of each other), or passive-aggressive behavior, which can all be quite detrimental to a marriage.[2]

One couple we know decided that they would assess each other's sexual boundaries based on a percentage method. If they both agreed that sexual intimacy sounded enjoyable, they would then communicate how much energy they could give to the sexual experience. If the number was low for a specific partner, say 25 percent, then the other person knew that there were limited kinds of sexual activity on the table. If it was a high percentage for both, say 80 percent, then they knew both spouses were up for trying new things or engaging in the sexual experience longer.

Cloud and Townsend also recommend spouses say yes out of love, not fear. Sex should be an act of love between partners—not something couples should engage in out of a fear of guilt, fear of a loss of love or loss of approval, or fear of a partner's anger.[3] Likewise, we would add to this that those individuals also say no out of love. Saying no can be an act of love because it is honest, it is your truth, and it communicates boundaries; and that is, itself, intimate. To feel emotionally safe and express your limits to your spouse is a gesture of love as well as is listening to your partner's boundaries, accepting them, and respecting them.[4]

Principle

At times, we may feel selfish when we establish boundaries in our relationships with others. After all, if Heavenly Father's second greatest commandment is to "love thy neighbour as thyself" (Matthew 22:39) and if we want to emulate the Savior, we are to serve others and strive to be selfless. None of us will ever find happiness if we are solely focused on ourselves; therefore, it is a delicate balance between setting boundaries to protect our own feelings and trying to make our partner happy too.

Selfishness can be defined as an attitude of being concerned with our own interests *above* the interests of others. Thus, selfishness is not about balancing both partners' wants, but instead only focusing on your own desires and believing they are more important than your partner's desires. Being selfish can include arrogance and conceit, vanity, an overly high opinion of oneself, or an effort to build yourself up while tearing your partner down.

When a spouse feels they cannot give themself fully to their partner physically, it is appropriate for him/her to pass on sexual intimacy and say no.

---

2 *See* Cloud and Townsend, *Boundaries*.
3 *See* Cloud and Townsend, *Boundaries*, 93–94.
4 *See* Cloud and Townsend, *Boundaries*, 74.

To be very clear, no means no. Even within marriage, consent must be given and is a priority to maintain intimacy and trust. Saying no to sex should result in the end of the discussion for that occasion. This does not mean that you might not feel bad for disappointing your partner; however, it is not a selfish act to take care of yourself, to be honest and transparent, and to be genuine and open with your partner about how you are feeling.

Nevertheless, some actions do fall under the umbrella of selfishness when it comes to the sexual relationship, such as when a spouse simply says no to sex and there is little effort made to come closer physically at all. Couples desire intimacy, they want to feel close to one another, and if it is not through sexual intimacy on that particular day, it can be through affection, positive communication, or shared time together.

In addition, selfishness occurs when a spouse manipulates or guilts their partner into having sex against their will. If one spouse feels like they cannot say no because of a sense of obligation or pressure by their partner, this leads to a dutiful or obligatory sexual relationship, which is often unfulfilling for *both* partners. Having sex in these circumstances pushes two people away from each other instead of bringing them closer together. Often, the partner who feels obligated into having sex resents their spouse, and it only causes the spouse to resist physical intimacy even more. In fact, such low-quality sexual relationships weaken the marriage and can lead to long-term emotional damage.

Explanation

There are numerous possibilities as to why a spouse may not desire physical intimacy on a given day. Here are several possibilities:[5]

1. **Expectations Concerning the Frequency of Sex in Marriage.** Over the years, we have met individuals—most often men—who believe that a sexual relationship should take place at least daily. Often misinformed peers or data that is gleaned from the internet or social media can give an individual the impression that sex is something that happens more frequently than it does. Such faulty high expectations can put too much pressure on a couple's sex life and increase conflict and hurt feelings. Wanting sex every day is perfectly fine, but expecting it is not.

2. **A Woman's Menstrual Cycle.** Sometimes a wife's menstrual period may last several days. For other women, the time frame may be much shorter or longer. In our counseling work, we have encountered several husbands who were quite impatient with their wives' menstrual cycles

---

5 Personal notes from Laura Brotherson.

because they were preoccupied with when they could have sex again. Insisting on sexual relations when a wife is going through a period, complete with cramps, bleeding, and general discomfort, is certainly not Christlike or a sign of respect. A husband should always place his wife's welfare above his own sexual desires.

3. **Physical Health Issues**. We are all susceptible to colds, allergies, aches, and pains. Moreover, in most instances, spouses who do not feel well are most often not in the mood to be romantic or sexual in any way. Therefore, when a spouse is sick, their partner should be focused on nursing them back to health and tending to their needs—not attempting to be physically intimate.

4. **Mental Health Issues.** Depression and anxiety (among other mental health challenges) may contribute to lessening a person's desire for sex as well. A symptom of depression is an inability to enjoy things a person typically enjoys, and sex can fall into that very category. Lower energy levels or mood swings may be associated with depression, and antidepressant medications can decrease a person's libido or ability to have an orgasm. Thus, mental health issues can directly affect sexual desire and sexual activity.

5. **Quality of the Marriage**. It is difficult for a wife to engage sexually with her husband when he is distant, unplugged as a father, or rude to her. Likewise, it is challenging for some husbands to want to be intimate with their spouse if she is critical of him, puts him down, or doesn't appreciate him. No one wants to be physically close to someone who treats them poorly or whom they don't trust. Emotional intimacy is as vital to a marriage as physical intimacy is.

6. **Fatigue.** Perhaps being tired or exhausted is the most common reason that prevents couples from engaging in sexual relations. When a partner is tired or exhausted, perhaps the best thing a loving spouse can do is tuck them into bed early, then take care of the children or other responsibilities so that their worn-out spouse can rest and be renewed. Physical intimacy will come on another day.

7. **Pregnancy.** Expecting a child brings many issues to bear besides a space problem in your living quarters. Generally, sex is comfortable and possible up until the later stages of the pregnancy. However, medical advice should be sought out in this situation. There are several factors to consider, including the baby's position, early bleeding, and how the wife feels in general. In most cases, a sexual relationship is

manageable if both spouses agree. Once again, husbands should be especially sensitive to their wife's body and sexual desires during this time.

8. **Children**. Often, one of the natural results of the sexual relationship is children. Over time, those babies grow up and become toddlers, preschoolers, and eventually, teenagers. When children are younger, they are often demanding and need constant attention. In many cases, just as a husband and wife begin snuggling together, a baby begins to cry or a toddler wakes up demanding a drink of water. When children become teenagers, they are often trying to balance homework, busy schedules, and late-night activities. They start to come into your bedroom later into the evening to talk and discuss important issues. These events are often disruptive to the sexual relationship between mom and dad and reduce opportunities for physical intimacy. Be understanding and patient. Meeting the needs of your children will often provide a better context for sex later with your spouse.

9. **Stress**. Even with the advances in technology, people are busier now than they ever have been before. Stress has been shown to lower sexual desire and interfere with physical intimacy. Stress creates an overwhelming feeling where people do not feel like they can focus or concentrate on one more thing. Because sex is a desire and not a need, sex often is put off to the side or ignored as stress levels rise.

10. **Body Image**. When a person has a poor body image and does not like their own body, sex does not sound appealing. A person may be uncomfortable being seen nude by their partner; therefore, he or she may avoid them. Experts have suggested seeing yourself naked and getting used to what you see in the mirror as a way to help a person accept themselves more fully. Taking a break from social media could also help you feel much better about your body image.

11. **Initiation/Timing.** How you initiate sex with your spouse and when you do it is particularly important. If your wife has requested to sleep in in the mornings due to being up late for work, initiating sex at 6:00 a.m. is a poor and inconsiderate decision. If your husband wants to be on time for lunch with an old high school friend, initiating sex before he walks out the door is not the best choice either. When you initiate sex, the timing of it matters. Do not set yourself up for failure; instead, set yourself up for success when it comes to the likelihood of

sex happening. Remember to pay attention to your partner and how they respond.
12. **Feeling Used.** No one wants to feel used, whether it is for selfish pleasure, trying to get pregnant, or otherwise. A spouse will become resentful and lose interest in sex if they feel their spouse is using them in any way. Sex is not pleasurable or desirable in this situation.
13. **Electronics.** Professionals have long recommended that couples should *not* have a television in their bedroom since it is a distraction to physical connection and intimacy. Additionally, we recommend that you do not have your phone in bed with you either. Electronics can get in the way of sex because other tasks become more important, and the electronic device receives all the attention instead of your spouse.
14. **Discomfort.** People may not want to have sex because it is uncomfortable to their bodies. If the sexual relationship causes consistent pain, you will most likely desire to stop. We recommend seeing a gynecologist or other doctor to make sure everything is functioning properly with your body. Furthermore, it might be important to check your hormone levels or anything else that can affect sexual desire physically.
15. **Unfair Distribution of Household Duties/Childcare.** If either spouse ignores the parenting responsibilities or household duties, intimacy may come to a halt rather quickly. Michelle Weiner Davis wrote, "Show me a woman who feels as if she's doing more than her fair share of housework or child care and I'll show you a woman who has more than her fair share of 'headaches.' Nothing turns a woman off quite as effectively as the feeling that she's doing most of the work at home . . . I can guarantee that you won't find her burning the midnight oil dreaming up ways to please her husband sexually . . .when a low-desire woman feels burned out, the first thing to go on her to-do list is sex."[6] Check in and make sure your partner is not feeling resentful about the distribution of responsibilities inside and outside the home, and make the necessary changes accordingly.

Practical Application

As you can see, there are many valid reasons (and probably many more we did not list) as to why a person may not be up for having sex with their

---

6   Michele Weiner Davis, *The Sex-Starved Marriage: Boosting Your Marriage Libido* (2003), 144–145.

spouse. While it is perfectly acceptable to say no, it's important to do it in a kind and respectful manner. There are many variations of saying no in a polite manner. Phrases such as these may work:

"I don't think so."
"Maybe. We will see later."
"Not tonight, but maybe tomorrow."
"That sounds really nice but [insert explanation]."

These statements are much more courteous in turning down the offer for physical intimacy, and they also communicate boundaries. Be considerate of your partner, and again, be careful to not to treat your partner as if he/she is annoying or exhausting you by asking to be close to you in a physical way. It is important to note that reframing your partner's advances as an attempt at positive connection is helpful. Likewise, partners can reframe dismissed advances not as personal rejection, but as a legitimate reason their partner is not in the mood.

Years ago in a marriage seminar, Doug shared a simple way to gauge your spouse's interests in a variety of things, such as what type of food she or he wants for dinner, to where he or she wants to go on vacation, to even having sex. He called it, "Scale of one to ten," in which husbands and wives rate their interests to each other on a scale of one to ten; ten being, *I am very interested*, and one being, *I am not interested at all*. For example, a husband could say, "Honey, on a scale of one to ten, how do you feel about eating Mexican food tonight at our favorite restaurant?" If the wife is at a seven or above, and the husband is too, then eating Mexican food sounds like a win-win. Likewise, the same questions could be asked about intimacy, movies, and other adventures. If a spouse were reporting a lower number, like a two or three, the next question would be, "What would it take to bring your three to an eight?" It is also perfectly acceptable for a spouse to say, "When it comes to intimacy, I am at a two right now, and I don't have the energy to change it." It does not hurt to ask as long as you are prepared to accept how your spouse responds, and inquiring can give you valuable information.

In addition, as we have stated previously, communication is vitally important in marriage and crucial when it comes to physical intimacy. A person should never fear voicing to his or her spouse that they are not interested in sex at that particular time; instead, they should have confidence that their boundaries will be honored. Likewise, when a person is interested in sex, they should feel comfortable conveying that message to their partner as well. Married couples ought to feel open and free to express their sexual desires to each other, just as they should politely turn down the offer of sex without judgment or reprimand.

Furthermore, try not to take offense or take it personally if your partner is not in the mood for physical intimacy. Respect the fact that sometimes "life happens," and *now* or *today* may not be the right time. It does not help increase sexual desire in your partner to play the victim, pout, withhold sex as revenge, give the silent treatment, or pull away emotionally (which we have seen more than once in our counseling offices). Couples would do well to identify their unmet desires and then go to work on the marriage, rather than sulk because they feel rejected sexually. Even more, connecting intimately does not have to be an all-or-nothing experience. Sometimes hugging, kissing, or cuddling can be enough to bond a couple together and help them feel close.

Lastly, if someone says yes when they really mean no, they are in a place of compliance, which is the equivalent of lying to their partner.[7] In other words, if your heart is not in it, then it's not a true agreement or real confirmation. This does not mean you only have sex when you're in the mood, but if you are open to that mood changing, give it a shot. If you know for sure that your desires or circumstances won't change, then set limits and tell the truth.

Love is a gift, not an obligation.[8] If your partner has demonstrated their love to you through their words or actions, such as service, gifts, or quality time, it does not mean you owe them anything in return, even physical intimacy. Loving each other does not imply you are indebted to each other, but instead, it's vital to share and receive love without requirements. In fact, the only expectation for love that is given between partners is gratitude.[9]

Cloud and Townsend write, "Boundaries are a 'litmus test' for the quality of our relationships."[10] So, if your partner respects the limits you set, then they are demonstrating that they value your desires and decisions. If your partner doesn't respect your boundaries, then it sends a message that they only love you when you acquiesce to their wants and desires. Total compliance in a marriage does not create a healthy relationship.[11] In fact, setting firm boundaries with your spouse and respecting those boundaries can lead to much greater intimacy overall.[12]

---

7   *See* Cloud and Townsend, *Boundaries*, 108.
8   *See* Cloud and Townsend, *Boundaries*, 120.
9   *See* Clark and Townsend, *Boundaries*.
10   Clark and Townsend, *Boundaries*, 110.
11   *See* Cloud and Townsend, *Boundaries*, 110.
12   *See* Clark and Townsend, *Boundaries*, 168.

Question #19:
What if I want to be intimate more often than my husband does?
Is that bad?

THERE IS NO BAD OR good when it comes to the desire to have sex. In fact, no two people will line up exactly the same on their desire for anything, whether it be chocolate cake, money, or sex! Attaching meaning of *good* and *bad* to the things we want creates shame. To be clear, wanting sex is not shameful; wanting sex more (or less!) than someone else is not shameful either. The desire is not the issue to consider here; however, what is important to consider is how we ask for sexual intimacy from our partner and how we react to our partner's response.

The question driving this chapter addresses the issue—what if a wife wants to have sex more than her husband? Is that a bad thing? To clarify, what this woman may be really asking is, "Is it unusual for a woman to want sex more than her husband?" In one study, researchers report that about 15 to 20 percent of women in marriages have a higher desire for sex than do their husbands.[1] That indicates that about one out of every five women have a stronger libido than their partner. We wouldn't say that makes it unusual per se but, rather, more uncommon. But again, just because fewer women have a higher sexual desire than their partner, that doesn't mean something is wrong or abnormal.

More specifically, this question opens the door to asking, how socially acceptable is it for women to want to be more physically intimate than men? In our American culture, there is certainly a stereotype that men are the sexual pursuers and women desire sex less frequently. For many generations, the concept of a sexually assertive woman would go against the grain or even be viewed negatively.

Who made the rule that women cannot be more interested in sex than men? Who decided that a wife must wait for her husband to make the first

---

1   Michael Sytsma, "When She Has the Stronger Sex Drive; Part One," *Shaunti Feldhahn* (Nov. 12, 2015), https://shaunti.com/2015/11/when-she-has-the-stronger-sex-drive-part-one/.

sexual move, and only then can she respond to his sexual advances? Many of these sexual expectations or rules have existed for centuries, but they do not necessarily reflect a healthy way of thinking or allow couples to navigate what works for them in their own sexual relationship.

Former BYU professor Dr. Brent Barlow explained,

> Some people cling to old stereotypes, mistakenly perceiving women as being less sexual than men. Not long ago I was invited to speak to a group of LDS married couples on the topic of sexuality in marriage. At the conclusion of my remarks one young wife asked, "Why is the sex drive so much stronger in men than in women?" I told the group I seriously questioned whether or not it was. For years it has been widely believed that men have the greater interest and drive towards sexual fulfillment. In addition, many women have been culturally conditioned to believe that their sexual inclinations are less than those of men—and if they are not, they should be or something is supposedly wrong. But recent research indicates that the capacity for sexual response in women is just as great, and in some cases even greater, than that of males. Recognizing this can help both partners be more aware of and sensitive to the other's desires and expectations.[2]

Consequently, husbands and wives will most likely have different levels of sexual desire throughout their marriage. As stated in a previous chapter, the word *drive* insinuates a vital need that a person cannot live without, such as food or sleep. Because a person does not need sex for survival, we prefer to use the term *sexual desire*, as it's more appropriate according to the latest research.[3] Overall, sometimes husbands will want sex more often than their wives, and at other times, wives may want sex more often than their husbands throughout their marriage.

Principle

You are a child of God. Knowing who we are and that we come from our Heavenly Father helps us to understand our divine nature. Part of life's journey is to learn to accept oneself and all of our shortcomings, for that matter. However,

---

2 Brent A Barlow, "They Twain Shall Be One Flesh," *Ensign*, Sept. 1986, 51.
3 Emily Nagoski, *Come As You Are: The Surprising New Science That Will Transform Your Sex Life* (2015).

we were created uniquely for a purpose that only we can fulfill; each of us is vital to His plan. Psalm 139:14 reads, "I will praise thee; for I am fearfully and wonderfully made; marvelous are thy works; and that my soul knoweth right well." Your body and spirit are brilliantly created to be yours. Own who you are—your thoughts, feelings, and desires—without shame.

It is important to point out that guilt and shame are distinctively different. Guilt is a feeling of "I did something bad," and shame means, "I am bad." Guilt comes from God, as that feeling compels us to change, repent, and make different choices. It leads us to want to be better so we don't feel that way again. With guilt, we believe we are inherently good but made a poor decision, or we understand that we have weaknesses and imperfections that we can improve upon.

Shame is defined as a belief that you are flawed, and therefore, *you are not worthy of love or belonging.*[4] Shame attaches negative meaning to the situation or to the choices you've made and attaches it to who you are as a person. Feeling ashamed develops into the belief that you are not good enough or worthy of change, and that you are your mistakes. While guilt is motivating, shame is debilitating.

We are all flawed, which is the reason we need our Savior, Jesus Christ, so that we may repent and become better. However, to lose hope that you can change, or to feel that you are not worthy of repentance, or that no one will love you because of your imperfections is truly defeating. Simply put, you are enough right now, no matter what. Too often, when it comes to women and sex, there is shame around every corner. For example:

- If I don't want sex with my husband tonight, I am a bad wife.
- If I don't want to try something new in the bedroom, I am a bad lover.
- If I don't want to have sex on the beach, I am uptight, unadventurous, and prudish.
- If I want sex and my husband declines, I must be unattractive.
- If I want sex more often than my husband does, something is wrong with me.

The list could go on; however, none of these statements is true. They are lies that interfere with the development of our own healthy sexuality. When it comes to sexual desire, there is no good or bad, and there should be no shame in owning what you want. For those whose sexual desires are not wholesome

---

4 See Brené Brown, *The Gifts of Imperfection: Let Go of Who You Think You're Supposed to Be and Embrace Who You Are* (2010), 39.

or not directed toward their spouse but toward another person, ecclesiastical advice or professional helps could assist an individual to stay on the right course.

Explanation

There are several factors that may contribute to a higher libido for women. First, hormone levels play a pivotal role in increasing one's sexual desire. Higher testosterone levels as well as estrogen levels, which rise before and during ovulation, increase sexual desire. On the other hand, increased amount of stress causes an increase in the hormone cortisol, which lowers libido. Because hormone levels vary from person to person and vary over the lifespan, sexual desire will fluctuate as well.

Second, the age of a woman impacts sexual desire. Research shows that women ages twenty-seven to forty-five are more likely to think about sex, have recurrent sexual fantasies, and have sex more often than women ages eighteen to twenty-six.[5] This may be because fertility is declining, and as women age, there is less chance of pregnancy and more openness to having sex.

Third, an increase in physical exercise or weight loss can increase libido. There is a positive correlation between an increase of physical activity and an increase in sexual desire. In fact, one study found that strengthening cardiovascular function can improve arousal, orgasm, and pleasure for women.[6] Also, a woman who feels good about herself physically and possesses self-confidence may be more apt to want more sex as well.

Practical Application

Shame is universal, and most of us feel uncomfortable talking about it, especially in the context of sex. However, as renowned shame researcher Brené Brown says, "The less we talk about shame, the more control it has over our lives."[7] Shame makes people feel isolated, trapped, and powerless, yet we all have the ability to develop shame resilience. Brown defines shame resilience as "the ability to recognize shame, to move through it constructively while

---

5 *See* J. A. Easton et al., "Reproduction Expediting: Sexual Motivations, Fantasies, and the Ticking Biological Clock," *Personality and Individual Differences* 49, no. 5 (2010): 516–520, doi:10.1016/j.paid.2010.05.018.

6 *See* L. M. Jiannine, "An Investigation of the Relationship between Physical Fitness, Self-Concept, and Sexual Functioning," *Journal of Education and Health Promotion* 7, no. 57 (2018), doi: 10.4103/jehp.jehp_157_17.

7 Brené Brown, *The Gifts of Imperfection: Let Go of Who You Think You're Supposed to Be and Embrace Who You Are* (2010), 38.

maintaining worthiness and authenticity, and to ultimately develop more courage, compassion, and connection as a result of our experience."[8]

To let go of society's cultural norms that create shame around sex, we will address four strategies on how to overcome shame itself:

1. **Recognize shame and understand your triggers.** It's helpful to identify how you feel shame in your body, such as a racing heartbeat, red cheeks, dry mouth, or a tightness in your chest, so you can know when you are feeling it and what brought it on. Through her research, Brené Brown identified twelve categories of shame triggers: money, work, family, parenting, motherhood/fatherhood, appearance and body image, mental and physical health, addiction, sex, surviving trauma, being stereotyped/labeled, aging, and religion. With sex being a trigger of shameful feelings, explore what messages and expectations around sex trigger shame for you.

2. **Practice critical awareness.** Identify the expectations in your life that create shame, whether they be from your family, society, church, or even from yourself. Then, reflect on whether those expectations are reasonable, healthy, or even realistic for you to attain, and if you don't meet those expectations, consider if they should be something you should feel ashamed of or not. Brené Brown likens critical awareness to "reality-checking" the messages that tell us that being imperfect means being inadequate.[9]

3. **Reach out and share your stories with people you trust.** The only way to lessen the shame is to be vulnerable and disclose the shame to someone who can be there for you and listen to it. Have courage and reach out to your trusted support system who are the people in your life who will not judge you and who can express love when you are feeling unlovable. Sharing your stories of shame increases the feelings of connection with others and a reassurance that you are not alone.

4. **Speak shame.** Speaking shame means to not back down from using the word *shame* and call it what it is. As scary as it feels to say it out loud, shame is not the same as feeling embarrassed or guilty; it goes much deeper than that. Remember, everyone feels shame; we just don't talk about it. Speaking shame means to talk about how you're feeling and ask for what you need from others.

---

8   Brown, *The Gifts of Imperfection*, 40.
9   Brown, *The Gifts of Imperfection*, 40.

In addition, an important component of shame resilience is empathy. While we need others to empathize with us when we feel shame, we need to be able to express empathy when they choose to share their shame stories with us too. Providing that safe place in marriage where your spouse can turn to you in their lowest moments and find compassion, reassurance, and acceptance creates more connection. Brown defines connection as "the energy that exists between people when they feel seen, heard, and valued; when they can give and receive without judgment; and when they derive sustenance and strength from the relationship."[10] Understanding your partner's feelings and making sure he or she feels loved even when they do not love themselves is essential.

Finally, whether it be a woman wanting sex more often than her husband or it being "bad" that one's sexual desire is high or low in general, shame is reduced in your marriage when you talk about it. Because shame thrives on secrecy and silence, be brave within your marriage and talk about the shame you might feel surrounding sex and other areas of your life when you feel it. This will open up authentic conversations, and it will allow you freedom in letting go of unnecessary expectations. Your sex life with your spouse is not about anyone else's or what society deems as "good," "bad," or "normal," but it's about you. Oscar Wilde once wrote, "Be yourself, everyone else is already taken."[11] Your partner married *you* for so many reasons, so live your life and not anyone else's . . . even in the bedroom.

---

10 Brown, *The Gifts of Imperfection*, 19.
11 Oscar Wilde, quoted on *Goodreads*, https://www.goodreads.com/quotes/19884-be-yourself-everyone-else-is-already-taken.

Question #20:
What if sex is painful or difficult for the woman?

Everyone's initial experience having sex is different and unique. When it comes to sex, there are many misconceptions, including that sexual intercourse will be painful for women. Initially, some women may experience minor pain or discomfort when they become sexually active, but it should not be considerably painful. Nevertheless, as many as 75 percent of women experience pain during sex at some point during their lives.[1] However, the good news is that in most cases, sexual pain and discomfort is usually temporary, improves with time, and can be resolved with medical intervention, if necessary. The hope is that sex is enjoyable, pleasurable, and connecting for couples.

Principle

Each person is a unique individual; therefore, we each have been created differently, and our bodies also greatly differ from one another's. Given that everyone is created differently, not everyone's body will respond to sex in the same way. For some, sex may be uncomfortable at first. For others, it may feel good immediately. Nevertheless, it is important to embrace your own personal experiences as a couple. There is no shame when it comes to how your body feels and what you prefer when it comes to sexual activity. Be careful not to judge your partner or make them feel as though something is wrong with them based on their sexual preferences. President Howard W. Hunter explained, "Tenderness and respect—never selfishness—must be the guiding principles in the intimate relationship between husband and wife."[2]

---

1 See "When Sex Is Painful," *The American College of Obstetricians and Gynecologists*, https://www.acog.org/womens-health/faqs/when-sex-is-painful.
2 *Teachings of Presidents of the Church: Howard W. Hunter* (2015), 215.

Both husband and wife will need to exercise patience as they explore each other's bodies and learn to meet each other's sexual desires.

Often, a husband or wife will compare aspects of their relationship to others around them, including the intimate life of their close friends or family members. It has often been said, "Comparison is the thief of joy."[3] When couples begin to compare their sexual experiences to others, or to what they have heard on television shows or read in magazines, it lowers their own sexual satisfaction. Even more, it can even negatively affect a person's libido.[4] The comparison trap sets couples up for failure because what they think is someone else's reality is very seldom accurate. In fact, the research shows that people are not completely honest when describing their own sexual experiences.[5] This may include whether sex creates initial discomfort or not. The truth is, your partner's body and desires are unique to them, and you are not in a relationship with anyone else. Thus, what is most important is focusing on each other, your own physically intimate experiences as well as your partner's, and the shared strengths in your relationship.

Explanation and Practical Application

From our research, it is evident that some people expect sexual intercourse to be uncomfortable or painful in the beginning. However, they may be unsure as to why that occurs. There are many potential causes for sexual discomfort, including both physical and psychological reasons.

Most women have a thin piece of tissue called a hymen located at their vaginal opening. The hymen differs in shape, and when it stretches or breaks, some women feel pain or discomfort, while other women do not feel it at all. In addition, the hymen can tear for numerous reasons, such as sexual activity, horseback riding, gymnastics, cycling, using tampons, or a gynecologist conducing a pelvic exam. There may even be temporary bleeding when this occurs.

In a previous chapter, we recommended scheduling a gynecological exam for women before they become sexually active. The exam can help a woman determine the size of her vaginal opening and the existence, shape, and condition

---

3   Quote attributed to Theodore Roosevelt, as cited by Joy D. Jones, "Value Beyond Measure," *Ensign* or *Liahona*, Nov. 2017.
4   *See* L. C. Day, A. Muise, & E.A. Impett, "Is Comparison the Thief of Joy? Sexual Narcissism and Social Comparisons in the Domain of Sexuality," *Personality and Social Psychology Bulletin* 43, no. 2 (2017): 233–244.
5   *See* Jeff Grabmeier, "Men, Women Lie About Sex to Match Gender Expectations," *EurekAlert!*, Ohio State University (28 May 2013), https://www.eurekalert.org/pub_releases/2013-05/osu-mwl052813.php.

of her hymen. It's also a great opportunity to ask a medical professional any general questions about sex. It also may be beneficial to obtain a series of dilators in order to stretch the vaginal opening in preparation for sexual intercourse. Additionally, certain sexual positions, deep penetration, or the penis hitting the woman's cervix can be uncomfortable or cause pain. The key is to go slow and find sexual positions that are comfortable, pleasurable, and work for you.

Another reason sex may be uncomfortable is due to vaginal dryness, especially for a woman's first sexual experiences. Typically, when a woman's body is sexually aroused, her vagina naturally lubricates itself. However, that is not always the case. Foreplay can help increase arousal levels in couples by kissing, touching, and other kinds of stimulation. In addition, many women experience vaginal dryness due to lower estrogen levels, especially in women who are postpartum or post-menopausal. The vaginal tissue becomes thin, dry, and less flexible, thereby increasing discomfort.

If a low amount of natural lubrication is produced, couples could use a synthetic lubrication that can assist with the ease of penetration and sexual intercourse. A study by Indiana University indicated that 70 percent of women who used lubricant during sex experienced an increase in pleasure and satisfaction.[6] There are many types of lubrication, including water-based, silicone-based, oil-based, and a hybrid of those. Emily Nagoski, sex educator and author, recommends silicone lubricants because they are long-lasting, safe to use with condoms, have a thicker consistency, which makes for less mess, are unlikely to cause an allergic reaction, and they dry to a silky powder finish.[7] You and your partner can pick out a few different lubricants to try and even bring a variety with you on your honeymoon to find the one that works best.

Occasional vaginal soreness is common and not something to be too concerned about when it comes to sexual intercourse. However, dyspareunia, which is the medical term for painful intercourse, or chronic genital pain, is rare and may be an indication that something is wrong. The pain may be contributed to vaginismus (painful vaginal contractions), vulvodynia (vaginal burning, stinging, or itching), pelvic floor dysfunction, bacterial infections (such as yeast infections), or the presence of ovarian cysts, fibroids, or endometriosis. If sexual pain persists and you begin to avoid sex altogether,

---

6 See Debby Herbenick, "Indiana U. at APHA: Studies About Why Men and Women Use Lubricants During Sex," *EurekAlert!*, Indiana University (Nov. 9 2009), https://www.eurekalert.org/pub_releases/2009-11/iu-iua_1110609.php#:~:text=An%20Indiana%20University%20study%20involving,of%20pleasurable%20and%20satisfying%20sex.

7 Emily Nagoski, *Come as You Are* (2015), 220.

it is an indication that it is time to consult a medical professional, such as a gynecologist.

Lastly, psychological issues, such as anxiety or low self-esteem, can impact a person's sexual discomfort. If a woman is nervous or anxious, it can cause her pelvic floor to tense up, which can be a barrier to intercourse. For men, anxiety and stress can lead to premature ejaculation. A warm bath or a massage can help couples relax before sex, and using birth control can also put couples more at ease if pregnancy is a concern.

Although sexual intercourse may be uncomfortable for some women, most discomfort diminishes over time as their bodies adapt to the experience. Persistence and a couple's mutual love for each other will help them learn how to make physical intimacy pleasurable for both partners. Keep in mind that sex should be pleasurable, and no one should have sex that is painful or uncomfortable.

Finally, women need to communicate openly and honestly with their partner about how sex feels concerning their own body. That means both the good and not-so-good, uncomfortable, or even painful. Let your partner know when they are doing something right and when they could be doing something differently that would feel better. Take responsibility for your own body and communicate in a positive way with your partner directly. Hopefully, no husband would ever intentionally want to cause physical or emotional pain to his new wife. If intercourse is uncomfortable or painful, couples should take additional steps to improve the situation, which may include slowing down, stopping, taking a break and trying again later, or focusing on what feels good instead of focusing solely on intercourse. Sexual intimacy should be enjoyable to both husband and wife; therefore, it is important to be patient and understanding with each other as couples work through any issues of discomfort together.

Question #21:
What if your spouse thinks sex is evil?

SEVERAL YEARS AGO, ONE OF us saw in our private practice a young woman who was recently married. This woman was convinced that sex was evil, wicked, vile, and something that women must simply "tolerate." She wanted little to do with her husband sexually, and he was quite frustrated. When the therapist asked the woman where her sexual beliefs came from, she explained her mother had told her often that sex was evil and vile. Unfortunately, this woman believed everything her mother had told her. This tendency to believe sex is evil may not be as uncommon as we think.

Many erroneous beliefs about sex are usually passed down from a myriad of sources, such as our family of origin, cultural values, societal implications, or even inaccurate messages from Church leaders and teachers. At times, these well-intended adults have had unfortunate or even abusive sexual experiences in their own personal lives. It could be possible that a father sends an erroneous message that sex is bad so that his children abstain from sex as teenagers. However, at the same time, his children associate shame and humiliation with sex. Perhaps a mother was sexually abused as a child and, consequently, has a poor opinion of sex and men; thereby, she creates a sense of fear of sex in her children. Maybe a wife is married to a selfish man who demands sex often and does not care if intimacy benefits her in any way, thus causing the sexual relationship to appear like a chore. Such experiences, and a host of many others, could be the catalyst for an individual teaching a child or others that sex is terrible or abhorrent or, at the minimum level, something that women must simply tolerate.

Marriage and family therapist Laura Brotherson has referred to the tendency to think so negatively about the sexual relationship as "The Good Girl Syndrome." Laura wrote,

> The Good Girl Syndrome is a result of the negative conditioning that occurs from parents, church, and society as they teach—or fail to teach—the goodness of sexuality and its divine purposes. This conditioning leads to negative thoughts and feelings about sex and the body, [often] resulting in an inhibited sexual response within marriage. . . . The Good Girl Syndrome may be the great underlying and underestimated cause of sexual dissatisfaction in marriage.[1]

Having a negative view of sexual relationships can be significantly damaging to married couples. Perhaps one of the best solutions to address this challenging mindset will be through the doctrines of the gospel of Jesus Christ and the plan of salvation.

Principle

False concepts and ideas can be unraveled by teaching true doctrine. President Boyd K. Packer stated, "True doctrine, understood, changes attitudes and behavior. The study of the doctrines of the gospel will improve behavior quicker than a study of behavior will improve behavior."[2] So, what is Church doctrine regarding the sexual relationship? Presidents of the Church, Apostles, other Church leaders, and even Brigham Young University professors have all taught the following principles:

- President John Taylor: "Well, [Heavenly Father] has planted, in accordance with this, a natural desire in woman towards man, and in man towards woman and a feeling of affection, regard, and sympathy exists between the sexes."[3]

- Sister Wendy Watson Nelson: "The Lord wants a husband and wife to partake of the wonders and joys of marital intimacy. Marital intimacy is ordained by God. It is commanded and commended by Him because it draws a husband and wife closer together, and closer to the Lord! True marital intimacy involves

---

1 Laura M. Brotherson, *And They Were Not Ashamed: Strengthening Marriage through Sexual Fulfillment* (2004), 2, 13.
2 Boyd K. Packer, "Little Children," *Ensign*, Nov. 1986, 17.
3 John Taylor, *Gospel Kingdom*, 61.

the whole soul of each spouse. It is the uniting of the body and the spirit of the husband with the body and the spirit of his wife."[4]

- Elder Hugh B. Brown: "The powerful sex drives are instinctive, which is to say, God-given, and therefore not evil."[5] Elder Brown also stated, "When the Lord established marriage—and He is its author—He made sex union lawful within that relationship, and it becomes both honorable and sanctified."[6]

- Chelom E. Leavitt: "Your Heavenly Father gave you a sexual nature and that He approves of sexual expression within marriage. When you use sexual expression in the context of a loving, committed marriage, these God-given desires create harmony and bond you to your spouse."[7]

- Joseph Fielding Smith: "The lawful association of the sexes is ordained of God, not only as the sole means of race perpetuation, but for the development of the higher faculties and nobler traits of human nature, which the love-inspired companionship of man and woman alone can insure."[8]

- Laura M. Padilla-Walker: "Sexuality is an inherent part of each child of God. We are created 'in the image of God' (Genesis 1:27), which means that our bodies, including our sexual organs, are a divine creation. Experiencing sexual feelings and sexual arousal is normal."[9]

- President Harold B. Lee: "Marriage is fraught with the highest bliss . . . The divine impulse within every true man and woman

---

[4] Wendy Watson Nelson, "Love and Marriage" (*An Evening with President Russell M. Nelson*, a worldwide devotional for young adults, Jan. 8, 2017), https://www.churchofjesuschrist.org/broadcasts/article/worldwide-devotionals/2017/01/love-and-marriage?lang=eng.

[5] Hugh B. Brown, *You and Your Marriage* (1979), 83.

[6] Brown, *You and Your Marriage*, 77.

[7] Chelom E. Leavitt, "Conversations about Intimacy and Sex That Can Prepare You for Marriage," *Ensign*: Digital Only: Young Adults, Aug. 2020, https://www.churchofjesuschrist.org/study/ya-weekly/2020/08/conversations-about-intimacy-and-sex-that-can-prepare-you-for-marriage?lang=eng.

[8] Joseph Fielding Smith, "Unchastity the Dominant Evil of the Age," *Improvement Era*, June 1917, 739.

[9] Laura M. Padilla-Walker and Meg O. Jankovich, "How, When, and Why: Talking To Your Children About Sexuality," *Ensign* or *Liahona*, Aug. 2020.

that impels companionship with the opposite sex is intended by our Maker as a holy impulse for a holy purpose—not to be satisfied as a mere biological urge or as a lust of the flesh in promiscuous associations, but to be reserved as an expression of true love in holy wedlock."[10]

- Ruth Lybbert Renlund and Elder Dale G. Renlund: "Our purpose in mortality is to become like our heavenly parents. Our divine understanding and use of sexual intimacy are essential to that process of becoming. . . . Heavenly Father intends that sexual relations in marriage be used to create children and to express love and strengthen the emotional, spiritual, and physical connections between husband and wife. In marriage, sexual intimacy should unite wife and husband together in trust, devotion, and consideration for each other."[11]

- President Spencer W. Kimball: "The Bible celebrates sex and its proper use, presenting it as God-created, God-ordained, God-blessed. It makes plain that God himself implanted the physical magnetism between the sexes for two reasons: for the propagation of the human race, and for the expression of that kind of love between man and wife that makes for true oneness. His commandment to the first man and woman to be 'one flesh' was as important as his command to 'be fruitful and multiply.'"[12]

It is very clear that the sexual relationship between husband and wife is God-ordained; God-sanctioned; and God-blessed—just as our prophets, leaders, and professionals have taught. Our Heavenly Father wants husbands and wives to have appropriate sexual relationships; He wants couples to bond through sexual intimacy. If someone is struggling with the mistaken belief that sex is bad, or even abhorrent, a good place to begin is to read and study these statements we have provided.

Explanation

One of the first commandments God gave to Adam and Eve was to "be fruitful, and multiply, and replenish the earth."[13] It would be impossible to

---

10 *Teachings of Presidents of the Church: Harold B. Lee* (2011), 112.
11 Dale G. Renlund and Sister Ruth Lybbert Renlund, "The Divine Purposes of Sexual Intimacy," *Ensign* or *Liahona*, Aug. 2020.
12 Billy Graham, "What the Bible Says About Sex," *Reader's Digest*, May 1970, 118, as quoted by Spencer W. Kimball, *Ensign*, May 1974, 7.
13 Genesis 1:28.

replenish the earth without marital intimacy. Remember, everything that comes from God is good, righteous, and certainly wholesome. Heavenly Father would not ask His children to participate in anything that is vulgar, wicked, or degrading. God created males and females so that they could ultimately have sexual relationships and bring children into the world. Moreover, after the creation, "God saw every thing that he had made, and behold, it was very good."[14] Note that everything our Father in Heaven created was not merely good, but *very good*. That is especially true of the creation of His sons and daughters, as well as every single part of our bodies—from our eyes to our ears; from our limbs to our internal organs; and from our sexual organs to our feet. Every part of our bodies is "very good."

Tim and Beverly LaHaye, authors of the classic book *The Act of Marriage*, have written, "God is the creator of sex. He set our human drives in motion, not to torture men and women, but to bring them enjoyment and fulfillment."[15] The LeHayes further explained, "What kind of God would go out of His way to equip His special creatures for an activity, give them the necessary drives to consummate it, and then forbid its use?"[16] As Latter-day Saints, we should recognize God's role and His approval of the sexual relationship. Similarly, Christian physician Dr. Ed Wheat explained, "You have God's permission to enjoy sex within your marriage. He invented sex; He thought it up to begin with."[17]

The sexual relationship is not merely for procreation, but also for enjoyment, bonding, healing, and for deep expressions of love between husband and wife. Furthermore, the sexual relationship between husband and wife should be viewed as healthy and wholesome—not bad, carnal, or evil. When the sexual relationship is set within the parameters the Lord has set, then sex can become one of the most bonding and uniting acts in which a married couple can participate. As Latter-day Saints, we should recognize that sexual relationships are not simply divinely approved, but divinely endorsed! Elder Parley P. Pratt explained, "The fact is, God made man, male and female; he planted in their bosoms those affections which are calculated to promote their happiness and union."[18] The sexual relationship between husband and wife

---

14   Genesis 1:31.
15   Tim LaHaye & Beverly LaHaye, *The Act of Marriage: The Beauty of Sexual Love* (1998), 20.
16   LaHaye & LaHaye, *The Act of Marriage*, 21.
17   Ed Wheat & Gaye Wheat, *Intended for Pleasure*, 4th ed. (2010), 18.
18   *Writings of Parley Parker Pratt*, ed. Parker Pratt Robison (1952), 52–53; as cited in the Eternal Marriage Student Manual; https://www.churchofjesuschrist.org/study/manual/eternal-marriage-student-manual/intimacy-in-marriage?lang=eng

should be the source of much happiness and fulfillment in marriage—not angst and turmoil.

Practical Application

If a spouse *does* feel that sex is bad or evil, then the other spouse can help. Together, the couple should spend some time studying the inspired words of prophets and apostles and other Church leaders to align their minds and hearts with gospel truths regarding sexual intimacy. There should be no harsh demands or using the scriptures to manipulate your partner during this process. However, couples would benefit greatly if they read talks and books together about sexual intimacy in order to become more comfortable. Education and information can certainly enhance sexual relationships.

Moreover, couples should also discuss their sexual beliefs together by asking questions such as the following:[19]

- How did you find out about sex? What was your reaction?
- How do you feel about sex? What are some of your thoughts about the sexual relationship?
- How did your parents talk about sex?
- Where did you learn your negative thoughts or impressions about sex?
- What do you feel is the purpose of sex in a relationship?
- Why do you think that it's important that we have a sexual relationship?
- What makes you uncomfortable about having sex? Is there anything I can do to make you more comfortable?

Couples should exercise patience and, at the same time, be understanding and strive to demonstrate empathy toward each other as they discuss these questions. We are aware of couples who struggled with some of these challenges. Yet, over time, they were able to resolve their differences and establish strong and healthy sexual relationships. Much of their success in overcoming these challenges was rooted in healthy, Christlike communication with each other.

Another useful tool to combat negative beliefs regarding sex would be to redefine what being "good" means.[20] Being "good" can include a person enjoying sex with his or her spouse. Affection, physical touch, pleasure, and orgasms

---

19 This list was compiled from multiple therapists, including Mark D. Ogletree, Kinsey Pistorius, and Laura Brotherson.

20 See Laura Brotherson, "The Good Girl Syndrome," *Strengthening Marriage.com* (Jul. 29, 2009), https://www.strengtheningmarriage.com/the-good-girl-syndrome/.

are all shared experiences within marriage that are good for the relationship. If there continue to be negative thoughts regarding sex, Laura Brotherson suggests repeating to yourself some positive affirmations about physical intimacy such as the ones listed below:[21]

- Sex is good.
- Sex is healthy and wholesome within marriage.
- I enjoy lovemaking.
- I feel loved when I am sexually intimate with my spouse.
- I am grateful for all parts of my body and my spouse's body.
- I am empowered when I fully engage in the sexual experience.
- I embrace my sexuality and enjoy expressing it.
- Sex is a natural and healthy part of a strong marriage.
- Sex is a way for me to express my love to my spouse.
- Our sexual relationship is important to me.

Affirmations help to retrain our negative thoughts into more positive ones, thereby changing behavior. Believing in the goodness of sex and allowing yourself to enjoy it, do it, and know the benefits of it can make all the difference in your approach to sex with your spouse.

Do not forget that there are many resources that can help you work through some of the deeper challenges that can be associated with a spouse not wanting to have a sexual relationship. Sometimes, parents or other family members can be a great source of information, empathy, and help. However, this issue could also lead to sexual aversion, which is a fear associated with sexual contact. Sexual aversion presents more like an anxiety disorder than a sexual disorder. It is treated through using relaxation techniques along with introducing the person to sexual stimuli slowly.[22] If this is more of what you or your partner is experiencing, then we recommend that you visit with a trained professional counselor who can provide insight, awareness, knowledge, and information that can be most helpful.

In our opening story for this chapter, we told the experience of the recently married young woman and her battle against the mistaken belief that sex is wicked and vile. Her therapist provided her with some good reading material and helped familiarize her with the teachings of the gospel on the subject of intimacy. Over

---

21 Personal notes from Laura M. Brotherson; *see also* Laura M. Brotherson, *From Honeymoon to Happily Ever After* (2019), 155–161.

22 *See* Cindy M. Meston, Alessandra Rellini, & Christopher Harte, "Sexual Aversion Disorder," *The Sexual Psychophysiology Laboratory: The University of Texas at Austin*, https://labs.la.utexas.edu/mestonlab/sexual-aversion-disorder/.

time, this young lady was able to change her mind, and her heart, and engage more fully with her husband in their intimate relationship. True doctrine can change attitudes and behavior. We have seen that miracle repeatedly.

Question #22:
What if pornography has been a problem for your fiancé(e) or spouse?

THE PREVALENCE OF PORNOGRAPHY HAS increased rapidly during the past several years. Truth be told, it is no longer an issue *if* a person will be exposed to pornography, but a matter of *when*. It will happen to you; it will happen to your children and those around them, even with all the protections in place. In 2008, more than 560 college students responded to an online survey:

- 93 percent of boys and 62 percent of girls were exposed to pornography before age eighteen.
- 14 percent of boys and 9 percent of girls were exposed to pornography before age thirteen.
- 69 percent of boys and 23 percent of girls have spent at least thirty consecutive minutes viewing internet pornography on at least one occasion.[1]

Further research indicates that by their senior year of high school, 100 percent of males have viewed pornography, and the average age of first exposure is eleven years of age.[2] Additionally, among young adults, ages eighteen to twenty-six, nearly nine out of ten (87 percent) young men and nearly one-third (31 percent) of young women report using pornography.[3] As a result, many bishops and stake presidents list pornography as their chief concern

---

1   *See* Chiara Sabina, Janis Wolak, and David Finkelhor, "The Nature and Dynamics of Internet Pornography Exposure for Youth," *CyberPsychology and Behavior* 11 (2008): 691–693.
2   *See* "Protecting Our Homes Against Pornography," *Church News*, Mar. 10, 2007.
3   *See* Jason S. Carroll, Laura M. Padilla-Walker, Larry J. Nelson, Chad D. Olson, Carolyn McNamara Barry, & Stephanie D. Madsen, "Generation XXX: Pornography Acceptance and Use Among Emerging Adults," *Journal of Adolescent Research*, 23, no. 1 (2008): 6–30.

for members of their wards and stakes. When a fiancé(e) or spouse learns of their loved one's pornography viewing, they may have significant difficulty in knowing what to do and where to go for help.

Many years ago, President Ezra Taft Benson declared, "The plaguing sin of this generation is sexual immorality."[4] He then went on to quote Joseph Smith, who explained that immorality "would be the source of more temptations, more buffetings, and more difficulties for the elders of [the Church] than any other" challenge.[5] We live in the day when this prophecy is being fulfilled before our very eyes. For those who struggle with the use of pornography—you are not alone. Many couples have experienced this challenge and, thankfully, have successfully navigated the treacherous waters.

Principle

The use of pornography is not a healthy practice, nor is it in harmony with keeping the commandments of the gospel of Jesus Christ. The healthy, God-given sexual desires designed as a blessing and bonding experience between a husband and wife can be warped into an unhealthy, out-of-control addiction. President Boyd K. Packer explained, "Addiction has the capacity to disconnect the human will and nullify moral agency. It can rob one of the power to decide."[6]

Like any other addiction, there are different degrees of pornography use that can range from accidentally stumbling onto it to compulsive viewing and masturbation that sometimes occurs multiple times daily. Pornography viewing is not merely a bad habit that can be overcome with some healthy goal-setting and a few spiritual interventions. Pornography is a drug, and many who view pornography regularly are just as hooked as any hard-core drug addict would be.

President Dallin H. Oaks explained:

> Pornography is also addictive. It impairs decision-making capacities, and it "hooks" its users, drawing them back obsessively for more and more. A man who had been addicted to pornography and to hard drugs wrote me this comparison: "In my eyes cocaine doesn't hold a candle to this. I have done both . . . Quitting even the hardest drugs was nothing

---

4 Ezra Taft Benson, "Cleansing the Inner Vessel," *Ensign*, May 1986, 4.
5 Ezra Taft Benson, *Teachings of Ezra Taft Benson* (1988), 277.
6 Boyd K. Packer, "Revelation in a Changing World," *Ensign*, Nov. 1989, 14.

compared to [trying to quit pornography]" (letter of Mar. 20, 2005).[7]

Sadly, when it comes to pornography use, the temptation can permeate all households, regardless of religious affiliation. According to a survey conducted by the Barna Group in the US in 2014:

- 64 percent of self-identified Christian men and 15 percent of self-identified Christian women view pornography at least once a month (compared to 65 percent of non-Christian men and 30 percent of non-Christian women).
- 37 percent of Christian men and 7 percent of Christian women view pornography at least several times a week (compared to 42 percent of non-Christian men and 11 percent of non-Christian women).[8]

Not every individual who engages in pornography is necessarily addicted. One key indicator of addiction is when the individual cannot stop, or abstain from, viewing pornography, or when sexual thoughts and ideas saturate their thoughts and feelings. In her book *The Porn Trap*, Wendy Maltz suggests five Cs for recognizing addiction: 1) psychological or physical *craving*, 2) *compulsion* to use pornography, 3) lack of *control* to avoid pornography, 4) *continue* to use or engage in the addiction, even though you know you should not, and 5) using or participating in the addiction, despite adverse *consequences*.[9]

Pornography is evasive and enticing because it stimulates the same pleasure hormones in the brain as sex does—dopamine for pleasure, norepinephrine that acts like adrenaline, oxytocin that increases bonding, and serotonin, which helps calm and relax the body.[10] In addition, pornography is easily accessible on the internet, free of cost, does not require a partner, and you can experience a sexual high, an increase in arousal, and a sexual release all while maintaining anonymity. Jeffrey Satinover further explained, "It is as though we have devised a form of heroin 100 times more powerful than before, usable in the privacy of one's own home and injected directly to the brain through the eyes. It's now available in unlimited supply via a self-replicating distribution network,

---

7   Dallin H. Oaks, "Pornography," *Ensign* or *Liahona*, May 2005.
8   See "Pornography Survey and Statistics," *Proven Men Ministries* (2014), http://www.provenmen.org/2014pornsurvey/.
9   See Wendy & Larry Maltz, *The Porn Trap: The Essential Guide to Overcoming Problems Caused by Pornography* (2008).
10 See Sam Black, "The Porn Circuit," *Covenant Eyes* (2021), 13, https://www.dioceseoflansing.org/sites/default/files/2017-03/The_Porn_Circuit.pdf.

glorified as art and protected by the constitution."[11] Except, it is not real. It leaves a person wanting more and more and is never truly satisfying. Exciting, maybe, but not satisfying.[12] True intimacy and satisfaction are experienced with real touch and an intimate connection by a real partner, not a fantasy.

Nevertheless, the temptation of pornography can override the truth. The men and women in the adult film and entertainment industry are frequently survivors of sexual abuse themselves and are coerced or forced to perform the sexual activity that is photographed or recorded. Additionally, pornographic images have been altered and enhanced, and they do not represent what real bodies or what real sex looks like. These images also contribute to sex trafficking all over the world.[13] There is also an increased drug use within the industry,[14] and actors often get high just to perform. Lastly, pornography includes repeated acts of sexual violence. A particular study reviewed 304 pornographic scenes and found that 88 percent contained physical aggression and almost half of the scenes contained verbal aggression, predominately name-calling.[15] Thus, pornography is a complete lie, devoid of any intimacy at all.

As a result, pornography use of any kind causes a loss of the Spirit of the Lord in the lives of those who engage in it; it leads to distorted feelings; it ruins relationships; and it exacerbates the loss of self-control and "nearly total consumption of time, thought, and energy."[16]

Elder Richard G. Scott explained,

> Satan has become a master at using the addictive power of pornography to limit individual capacity to be led by the Spirit. The onslaught of pornography in all of its vicious, corroding, destructive forms has caused great grief, suffering, heartache, and destroyed marriages. It is one of the most damning influences on earth. Whether it be through the printed page, movies, television, obscene lyrics, vulgarities

---

11 Jeffrey Satinover, as cited in *He Restoreth My Soul* (2010), 49.
12 *See* Black, "The Porn Circuit."
13 *See* Black, "The Porn Circuit."
14 *See* "UCLA Study Finds that Porn Stars Have STDs, Use Drugs," *CW 39*, June 13, 2014; https://cw39.com/cw39/ucla-study-finds-that-porn-stars-have-stds-use-drugs/.
15 *See* A. J. Bridges et al., "Aggression and Sexual Behavior in Best-Selling Pornography Videos: A Content Analysis," *Violence Against Women*, 16, no. 10 (Oct. 2010), doi: 10.1177/1077801210382866.
16 Linda S. Reeves, "Protection from Pornography—a Christ-Focused Home," *Ensign* or *Liahona*, May 2014.

on the telephone, or flickering personal computer screen, pornography is overpoweringly addictive and severely damaging. This potent tool of Lucifer degrades the mind and the heart and the soul of any who use it. All who are caught in its seductive, tantalizing web and remain so will become addicted to its immoral, destructive influence. For many, that addiction cannot be overcome without help. The tragic pattern is so familiar. It begins with curiosity that is fueled by its stimulation and is justified by the false premise that when done privately, it does no harm to anyone else. For those lulled by this lie, the experimentation goes deeper, with more powerful stimulations, until the trap closes and a terribly immoral, addictive habit exercises its vicious control.[17]

Explanation

The consumption of pornography has numerous damaging effects. Instead of connection and intimacy between partners, pornography focuses on oneself and fosters self-centered behaviors.[18] Elder Richard G. Scott wrote, "Participation in pornography in any of its lurid forms is a manifestation of unbridled selfishness." He goes on to say that there is "emotional and spiritual damage . . . caused by such abhorrent activity."[19] Upon the discovery of a spouse's sexual addiction, partners of sex addicts have shared feelings of "hurt, betrayal, rejection, abandonment, devastation, loneliness, shame, isolation, humiliation, jealousy, and anger, as well as loss of self-esteem."[20] In addition, Steffens and Rennie studied partners of sex addicts and found that 70 percent suffered from symptoms of post-traumatic stress disorder (PTSD) after their partner disclosed their addiction and that it triggered a significant attachment injury to the relationship.[21]

Often, partners of sex addicts take their spouse's pornography addiction personally, comparing themselves to the online images their spouse may be viewing. They will ask themselves questions such as these: Are they not good

---

17 Richard G. Scott, "To Acquire Spiritual Guidance," *Ensign* or *Liahona*, Nov. 2009.
18 *See* Black, "The Porn Circuit."
19 Scott, "To Acquire Spiritual Guidance."
20 Schneider, J. P., "Effects of Cybersex Addiction on the Family: Results of a Survey," *Sexual Addiction & Compulsivity* 7 (2000): 31.
21 *See* Barbara A. Steffens and Robyn L. Rennie, "The Traumatic Nature of Disclosure for Wives of Sexual Addicts," *Sexual Addiction & Compulsivity*, 13 (2006): 260, 263.

enough? Are they not attractive enough? Why do their spouses no longer find them sexually desirable? Are they not having enough sex? It is important for the partners of sex addicts to know that their spouse's pornography addiction is not their responsibility. They did not cause it, nor can they alleviate it. Many sex addicts have had this addiction long before they even met their spouses, and they think getting married and having sex will put an end to it. However, it does not.

Recently, university professors Brian J. Willoughby, Galena Rhoades, and Jason Carroll reported some research on pornography and its impact on marriage. Among their findings, they shared the following:

- **There is certainly a gender gap when it comes to pornography viewing.** This study reported that among those in dating relationships, 36 percent of women reported never viewing pornography, compared to 19 percent of men. Among married women and men, 51 percent of women and 25 percent of men reported never viewing pornography. Therefore, a higher percentage of men view pornography than women.
- **Pornography viewing is most common among young men.** In this study, researchers reported that 17.3 percent of men under thirty years of age view pornography daily, compared to 6.9 percent of men over thirty years of age.
- **One in five couples reports conflict related to pornography.** Their research documented that one in four men actively hide their pornography viewing from their partner, and one in three women are concerned about their partner's pornography viewing.
- **Pornography is associated with lower relationship quality.** Couples where neither partner uses pornography reported the highest levels of relationship quality. In fact, there was a consistent reduction in relationship stability, commitment, and satisfaction when pornography rates were higher among couples. Put another way, the more a partner engaged in pornography use, the lower the quality of the marriage relationship.[22]

In addition, engaging in pornography use decreases sexual satisfaction. In fact, the pornography user tends to be less satisfied with the relationship,

---

22   *See* Brian J. Willoughby, Galena K. Rhoades, and Jason S. Carroll, "The Porn Gap: How is Pornography Impacting Relationships Between Men and Women Today?" *A Report from the Wheatley Institution* (2021); https://wheatley.byu.edu/00000183-2328-dc42-a7f7-7ba86d810001/the-porn-gap.

their partner's affection, and their physical appearance too.[23] Men who engage in pornography are also more likely to experience erectile dysfunction and discover that they can only achieve an erection while viewing pornography.[24] As a result, a couple may have sex less often because the pornography user loses interest in their partner as their interest in looking at pornography increases.[25]

Furthermore, other effects of pornography include the following:
- poor sexual conditioning and unrealistic expectations for real, intimate relationships
- objectifying others and using them for personal gratification
- weakening of the foundation of trust and emotional safety between spouses in marriage due to dishonesty and deception
- wounding of the emotional connection between husband and wife vital for a healthy sexual relationship
- decreasing of the mental and emotional well-being of both partners
- exacerbating of insecurities; creating an obsessive focus on sex in the marriage
- often creating patterns of interacting that are manipulative, blaming, and justifying to cover the shame and denial partners struggling with pornography may be feeling.[26]

Pornography use can create a fantasy of imitating viewed images or video, which can lead to acting it out with additional partners. In fact, the consumption of pornography has been known to increase infidelity by 318 percent.[27] Partners of sex addicts report that their spouse's internet affairs were as emotionally hurtful as relationships outside the marriage that were not conducted online.[28] Two Latter-day Saint scholars and pornography researchers, Rory C. Reid and Jill C. Manning, have shared their opinion that any form of pornography use is a form of infidelity. They explained,

---

23 *See* Dolf Zillmann and Jennings Bryant, "Pornography's Impact on Sexual Satisfaction," *Journal of Applied Social Psychology*, 18 (1988): 438–453.
24 *See* B. Y. Park et al., "Is Internet Pornography Causing Sexual Dysfunctions? A Review with Clinical Reports," *Behavioral Sciences* 6, no. 3 (2016): 17, https://doi.org/10.3390/bs6030017.
25 *See* Zillman and Bryant, "Pornography's Impact."
26 *See* Mary Anne Layden, "Pornography and Relationship Damage Research," *Porn Harms Research* (December 13, 2013), https://pornharmsresearch.com/2013/12/talking-points-pornography-and-relationship-damage-research/.
27 *See* Black, "The Porn Circuit."
28 *See* Steffens and Rennie, "The Traumatic Nature of Disclosure."

Pornography consumption of any kind constitutes a form of infidelity. Emotional fidelity, a commitment of heart and mind, is undermined by the consumption of pornography as thoughts and feelings turn from one's spouse toward objects, people, or practices outside the marriage covenants. Breaches of fidelity, both emotional and physical, destroy trust, respect, and marital intimacy on all levels. Such breaches threaten the stability of marriages, families, and communities.[29]

Furthermore, the American Academy of Matrimonial Lawyers surveyed 350 divorce lawyers and found that 56 percent of divorces entailed one person having a preoccupied interest in pornographic websites.[30] Thus, pornography's effects on a marriage can be truly devastating, even being a catalyst that ends the marriage altogether.

Practical Application

Addiction is often a result of disconnection. When people feel disconnected from others, they search to find something that relieves their discomfort. Mark Bird, a leading therapist and researcher in the field of sex addiction, writes that pornography is a symptom of what he terms "connective disorders" and that people use pornography (or other common addictive behaviors, such as alcohol, drugs, nicotine, sex, gambling, food, pain killers, etc.) to fill the void of the disconnection.[31]

As such, viewing pornography, along with masturbation, becomes an unhealthy coping mechanism that people use when they are trying to manage the negative feelings of disconnection. Often, this disconnection is not only with a spouse, but with many others, including friends, family, coworkers, church members, and neighbors. Moreover, whether participation in pornography is to reduce stress or anxiety, combat loneliness and depression, or even cope with rejection from a spouse, this unhealthy coping skill becomes a crutch. Instead, it is vital to develop healthier ways to manage negative emotions and increase connection between spouses.

---

29 Rory C. Reid & Jill C. Manning, "Overcoming the Destructive Influence of Pornography," in *Helping and Healing Our Families* (2005), 103.
30 *See* J. Manning, *Senate Testimony 2004*, referencing J. Dedmon, "Is the Internet Bad for Your Marriage? Online Affairs, Pornographic Sites Playing Greater Role in Divorces," 2002, press release from The Dilenschneider Group, Inc., 14.
31 *See* Mark H. Bird, *In Tandem: Recovering Me, Recovering Us*, (2017), 18–19.

Couples who are most often successful in working their way through a pornography addiction work on the addiction as a team. Consider the following suggestions:

For the Pornography/Sex Addict
1. Take accountability by acknowledging your part. Admit you have a problem without minimizing its effects on your marriage and your spouse, not justifying or seeking to excuse the negative behavior, but instead, own that you have a problem and the damage that it has caused.
2. Demonstrate empathy toward your partner.[32] Validate his or her feelings, as there are many fears and other feelings that need to be heard.
3. Use interventions that help reduce temptation. Getting pornography out of your life includes burying your weapons (Alma 24:19), including your electronic devices. After all, if you were an alcoholic, it would be difficult to stop drinking if you worked in a bar. Likewise, most sex addicts are surrounded by phones, computers, tablets, and other gadgets that provide easy access to pornography. Set up boundaries, such as not taking electronic devices into the bathroom, upstairs, or to any room of the house where you are alone; maintaining open-door policies with computer screens; placing internet filters and accountability software on phones and tablets; and disabling the home internet at a certain time each night. Often, in counseling settings, these suggestions are often met with much resistance, yet it is very simple. Stay far away from the source of temptation, and be willing to do what it takes to ensure safety for your marriage and family.
4. Participate in a 12-Step Addiction Recovery Program. Such programs are typically facilitated by those who have maintained a level of sobriety from the addiction for a significant period, and others who are dealing with the addiction attend the meetings. People experience great strength and resolve in the addiction recovery meetings while gaining a much-needed support system. You can find these resources at addictionrecovery.lds.org.
5. Identify a sponsor or accountability partner. "Sponsors" are individuals who have navigated their way successfully through the addiction

---
32 *See* Bird, *In Tandem*, 2017.

program and are able to help, give counsel, and serve as lifelines when you or your spouse is struggling. Mainly, these are individuals whom an addicted spouse would report to each week, check in with, and receive valuable counsel and practical ideas from.
6. Seek a well-qualified and trained therapist. Professional counseling can also be extremely helpful to provide the necessary tools to cope with the pornography addiction. Specifically, a certified sex addiction therapist may help you to construct an inventory, process the past and connect it to the present, identify triggers, set boundaries, and provide helpful resources. In addition, a couple's therapist can help a husband and wife navigate the effects of the pornography addiction on their relationship.
7. Fortify yourselves spiritually. Stand in holy places. Immerse yourself in the scriptures, read the words of living prophets, listen to conference talks and inspiring music, and build your foundation on our Savior, Jesus Christ. As you strive to feel the presence of the Holy Ghost more in your life, you will feel stronger to withstand temptation.

For the Partner of the Pornography/Sex Addict
1. Manage your own emotions.[33] Identifying your triggers helps to understand the intense emotions you may feel as you navigate this process. It takes practice to learn how to regulate our emotions and be able to feel them and share them but not lose control. Make sure you are making a list of coping skills for yourself and using them when you feel emotionally flooded and overwhelmed.
2. Allow your partner the space to do their own work. You might think it's your job to monitor your spouse's addictive behavior and/or relapses, but it's not. You do not want to go down the trail of monitoring phones and devices and checking on your spouse constantly. We have found it weighs heavily on a spouse to take on that responsibility, and it results in an overwhelming level of disappointment. In addition, this dynamic will most likely create further secrecy and withdrawal from the sex addict, and transparency in the marriage will be difficult to achieve. Allow your partner to work on his or her program and have patience as they learn new strategies to overcome their pornography use.

---

33 See Bird, *In Tandem*, 2017.

3. Attend a support group. Support groups help you rub shoulders with other spouses who are encountering the same challenges and who need support. There is great strength that you can tap into as you listen to the success stories of those who have been through this addiction as well as those whom you can relate to, empathize with, and comfort through this shared challenge.
4. Find an individual therapist for you. Due to the shame that comes with having a partner who struggles with pornography use, it might be difficult to find people you trust to talk about what you are experiencing. Therefore, finding your own support system is imperative. Individual therapy provides that confidential and safe place for you to process your thoughts and feelings without judgment.

For Couples
1. Be honest. Share your thoughts and feelings with each other, and be truthful about your actions. Show each other that you value transparency in your relationship by not keeping secrets.
2. Communicate effectively. Engage in time-outs, practice reflective listening, use "I" statements, speak with respect, and validate one another's feelings.
3. Create safety.[34] Because there is a lack of trust in the relationship, couples must rebuild their sense of emotional safety. So, try to be supportive, recognize and manage your own intense emotions, identify triggers in yourself and in your partner, and respond with empathy toward each other.
4. Build positive experiences.[35] Due to the anxiety and stress that addiction can bring into a marriage, it is even more important to have shared positive experiences together. Thus, implement the things that bring positivity and connection to your relationship and create opportunities to experience them.
5. Engage in couple therapy.[36] Mark Bird has written, "Couple therapy can provide opportunities to change couple patterns in a way that lowers emotional reactivity. Being able to create mutual understanding and accountability around these healthier patterns is critical in helping

---

34 *See* Bird, *In Tandem*, 2017.
35 *See* Bird, *In Tandem*, 2017.
36 *See* Bird, *In Tandem*, 2017.

individual recovery changes solidify more quickly, which in turn helps your relationship improve."[37]

When we turn our whole souls to Jesus Christ for help and healing, He strengthens and refines us as we learn and grow through our challenges. In Ether 12:27 we read:

> And if men come unto me I will show unto them their weakness. I give unto men weakness that they may be humble; and my grace is sufficient for all men that humble themselves before me; for if they humble themselves before me, and have faith in me, then will I make weak things become strong unto them.

Weaknesses can become strengths. Our moral temptations and difficulties provide opportunities for us to turn to our loving Father in Heaven with a broken heart and contrite spirit.[38] Pride and self-will are some of the grave consequences of the natural man. While the Lord can perform miracles and remove any cross from our lives, He has a perfect understanding of what is required of us in our eternal growth and development and that making our lives free from difficulties would not allow us to ultimately reach our full potential and receive eternal joy.

There is hope that we can overcome something even as reprehensible as compulsive sexual behaviors—including pornography consumption and masturbation. We may question if it really is possible to heal from addiction and recover from the associated emotional pain and trauma. Like Nephi, we may cry out from the depths of our souls,

> I am encompassed about, because of the temptations and the sins which do so easily beset me. And when I desire to rejoice, my heart groaneth because of my sins; nevertheless, I know in whom I have trusted. My God hath been my support; he hath led me through mine afflictions in the wilderness; and he hath preserved me upon the waters of the great deep. He hath filled me with his love, even unto the consuming of my flesh.[39]

---

37 *See* Bird, *In Tandem*, 2017, 168.
38 *See* 2 Nephi 4:32 and 3 Nephi 12:19.
39 2 Nephi 4:18–21.

We can trust in God's great and infinite love, wisdom, and power to refine us through our human weaknesses and draw us unto Him continually. The Lord loves all His children, including those who are addicted to pornography and other afflictions. He is waiting to help heal our hearts and our souls. In Jesus Christ is where individuals will find strength and power to resist temptation and truly change. In fact, "Only in Christ is there power to transform the human mind and the human heart. . . . Only in Jesus Christ can any man learn the truth of what he is and how he can be changed from what he is to do the good for which he hopes."[40]

---

40 *Gospel Doctrine Manual,* "In His Steps Today" (1969), 4.

Question #23:
How do you get over the feeling that all your husband wants to do is have sex?

THIS QUESTION IS OFTEN POSED by newly married women. However, let's not suggest that it can't be the experience of men as well. The sexual journey for Latter-day Saint newlyweds can be filled with surprises; after all, this is most likely brand-new territory for both husbands and wives. In most cases, men and women have gone from their premarital years of trying to live the law of chastity, where sexual relationships are prohibited, to their newly married life of frequent affection and sexual relations. Of course, there will be challenges to navigate and new experiences to share.

In previous chapters, we addressed issues of sexual desire and frequency. Because more men experience spontaneous desire, it can be common for new brides to feel that all their husbands want to do is have sex. In fact, the sexual relationship is something that many young men have heard about for a long time, and many have had to "bridle their passions," so to speak. Now that they can share in sexual intimacy with their wives, some men may find it difficult to control their passions, while at the same time considering the feelings and needs of their wives. Therefore, it may appear to women that their husbands have sex on their minds continuously.

Other ways in which a person may feel that their spouse is fixated on sex is if their spouse talks about sex a majority of the time and not much else; focuses a lot of attention on their partner's looks and comments constantly on their body; minimizes or dismisses the couple's sexual experiences they do have; criticizes or insults a partner for their efforts in the bedroom; compares their sex life to others' as a way to express dissatisfaction; or grabs/gropes or touches private areas without consent or as the only way to show physical affection. In a counseling session once, a wife shared that she routinely scratched her husband's back before bed each night as a way to express love and affection and increase closeness between them. However, as her husband rolled over to go to sleep, he would put his arm around her and rest it on her breast. She expressed that this was not comfortable for her and that she didn't feel her husband could show her affection without touching the private parts of her body. The wife shared the disappointment she felt that her husband didn't ask her if she wanted a back scratch in return or that he didn't ask how he could show her affection and make her feel loved at all. Instead, she admitted that she withdrew from her husband, and the lack of nonsexual touch in her marriage made her feel more distant from him instead of creating a closer connection as it is intended.

When it feels like all a spouse wants to do is have sex, there may be a need for increased intimacy within the marriage. Often, through media sources or cultural beliefs, a person may believe sex and intimacy are the same thing. However, that is not the case. Sex is only a part of one type of intimacy within a relationship. So, when it feels like a spouse is only focusing on one way to connect, which may be sex, it often means there is a lack of focus on other types of intimate connection. Different types of intimacy within marriage include physical, emotional, intellectual, experiential, and spiritual. Increasing each type of intimacy within the relationship will allow both partners to feel more fulfilled and that sex is not the only way for a couple to connect.

Principle

Share your testimony of the gospel of Jesus Christ with your spouse. Spiritual intimacy is one facet of marital intimacy, just as physical intimacy or sex is. Connecting on a spiritual level with your spouse is important for couples, as it includes sharing spiritual journeys and faith with each other without judgment. Simply because an LDS couple chooses to get married in the temple and be sealed for time and all eternity doesn't mean they are spiritually connected. Research has shown that couples who attend religious services together are more satisfied with their marriage. In addition, the more often husbands attend religious services, the more wives report a higher level of happiness and an increase in affection, understanding, and time spent together.[1] More specifically, couples who experience spiritual intimacy within their marriage report an increase in warmth toward one another, more humor and love in the relationship, and less negativity or hostility toward

---

1 W. Bradford Wilcox, "Soft Patriarchs and New Men: How Christianity Shapes Fathers and Husbands," *University of Virginia Arts & Sciences* (2004); https://sociology.as.virginia.edu/soft-patriarchs-and-new-men-how-christianity-shapes-fathers-and-husbands.

their spouse.[2] Thus, as a couple connects on a spiritual level, they can greatly enhance their relationship and marital functioning.

Elder Craig C. Christensen stated, "Some speak of a testimony as if it were a light switch—it's either on or off; you either have a testimony, or you do not. In reality, a testimony is more like a tree that passes through various stages of growth and development."[3] If our own testimonies of the gospel of Jesus Christ are ever changing, growing, strengthening, or even weakening at times, it is important to share that journey with your partner. When we engage in this conversation, it is deep, it is personal, and it provides connection when we reveal our faith in our Heavenly Father and His son, Jesus Christ, to our spouse. Moreover, spiritual connections with a spouse can also lead to connections in other aspects of marital intimacy.

Explanation

Sex is a powerful sensory and emotional experience for both husband and wife. Generally, during sexual intercourse, husbands have little trouble reaching a climax compared to their wives. Therefore, it is easy for men to equate sex and intimacy. For many men, sexual relations are an expression of love, yet women need more to feel loved than simply physical intimacy alone. Besides, physical intimacy goes beyond just sex. Physical intimacy consists of any type of touching, kissing, hugging, cuddling, holding hands, massaging, embracing one another, and sex. Sex is only a part of physical intimacy within marriage, and touch and affection are crucial to building a connection between partners. If your partner doesn't touch you other than to have sex, you may feel like that is all your spouse wants.

Emotional intimacy is essential within the marital relationship and involves eye contact, listening to your partner, validating their feelings, empathizing, acknowledging each other, showing interest, checking in, and asking questions. Couples strengthen their emotional intimacy when they share their feelings, their hopes, dreams, fears, and personal experiences. As spouses turn toward each other emotionally, their bond deepens. Brigham Young University family science scholars Stahmann, Young, and Grover have explained, "We believe that most husbands wouldn't have to talk their wives into sexual relations if

---

2   "Spiritual Intimacy: Talking as 'Soul Mates,'" Bowling Green State University, College of Arts and Sciences; accessed 19 Oct. 2023, https://www.bgsu.edu/arts-and-sciences/psychology/graduate-program/clinical/the-psychology-of-spirituality-and-family/research-findings/marriage-couples/spiritual-intimacy.html
3   Craig C. Christensen, "I Know These Things of Myself," *Ensign* or *Liahona*, Nov. 2014.

they would provide what their wives long for most: emotional intimacy in the areas of trust, tenderness, caring, acceptance, and good communication. Women need to feel loved and nurtured before they can begin to be aroused and develop desires for sexual intimacy. For women, emotional intimacy is at least as important as the act of having sex."[4]

Intellectual intimacy, or brain-to-brain connection, consists of having deep conversations over complex topics, such as religion, politics, parenting, cultural norms, finances, education, career opportunities, and open discussions regarding your beliefs or your opinions with your spouse. Intellectual intimacy does not mean that a husband and a wife need to agree on everything to achieve an increased closeness. However, it does infer respect, no judgment, an exchange of information, and possibly even challenging each other's thoughts or beliefs because it's safe to do so. Men and women both need to feel intellectually stimulated in a partnership and possess a freedom to think for themselves.

Experiential intimacy consists of shared experiences and activities that you enjoy together as a couple. For example, going on dates either by yourselves or with other couples, watching sports together or various TV shows you like to watch together, taking dance classes, vacationing together, or attending events, such as concerts, movies, art shows, etc. Any shared activity you and your spouse enjoy and spend time doing together helps to increase intimacy within your marriage. It requires putting aside time and prioritizing your relationship, and it provides common ground that connects you and your partner together.

Practical Application

The expression of love is not limited to the bedroom, and the overall fulfillment in marriage involves other experiences in life. Couples should discuss what intimacy means to each of them, including physical, emotional, intellectual, experiential, and spiritual intimacy. There should be areas of your lives and in your relationship where sex is not the predominant theme. If you want to show your spouse that there is more on your mind all day than sex, consider strengthening additional facets of intimacy in your marriage, including the following:

Spiritual Intimacy
Strengthening spiritual intimacy includes recognizing and discussing blessings that occur throughout the day, praying together, attending Church and

---

4 Robert F. Stahmann, Wayne R. Young, & Julie G. Grover, *Becoming One: Intimacy in Marriage* (2004), 14–15.

the temple together, reading scriptures together, supporting one another in callings, sharing inspirational talks from Church leaders, asking for/giving/receiving priesthood blessings, and applying the Atonement of Jesus Christ to your marriage by exercising repentance and forgiveness in your relationship. Even more, as you share your personal testimonies of Jesus Christ, your own spiritual experiences, the whisperings of the Holy Ghost in your life, the answers to your prayers, your questions and doubts, and the conviction of your beliefs with your spouse, it will bring you closer together. Spiritual intimacy is truly giving your partner spiritual support in your marriage.

Physical Intimacy
Improving physical intimacy begins with focusing on nonsexual touch or affection. Physical touch releases the hormone oxytocin which helps to reduce stress and bond two people together. It also facilitates a stronger and more secure attachment between partners. Experts suggest couples engage in a six-second kiss every day,[5] greet and depart from each other with a sign of affection, make eye contact and hold each other's gaze, give massages, hold hands in the car, and cuddle on the couch, among many other ways to show affection. Ask your partner what his or her favorite way to feel loved through touch is, and make an effort to do it more often. Also, touch between partners does not begin at midnight in the bedroom—it starts in the morning and continues throughout the day.

In addition, you should not necessarily pursue a sexual relationship with your spouse every time you desire it any more than you should shove food into your mouth each time you think about your favorite snacks. If you can sense that your spouse is reluctant to engage in sex, back off, give them some space, and respect their feelings. Practice self-control and discipline as you learn to accept your partner. Learn to love your spouse where they are at and accept what they can give physically, even if it is not sex at that time.

Emotional Intimacy
Emotional intimacy is defined as mutual self-disclosure; therefore, both partners need to be willing to express their feelings, not just facts. Sharing emotions creates a deep, meaningful connection where couples can move beyond superficial discussions. It is helpful to be able to identify your own feelings or be able to help your partner identify theirs; however, be honest,

---

5   *See* Kari Rusnak, "The Six Second Kiss," *The Gottman Institute,* July 1, 2021; https://www.gottman.com/blog/the-six-second-kiss/.

transparent, be curious and ask questions, express appreciation, and compliment one another. Another way to strengthen emotional intimacy is through reflective listening, which is when one partner reflects back to the other what they heard their partner say. Summarize what was shared with no judgments or assumptions, and simply say what you heard. Do not ask questions or state your opinion at this time. Restating what was shared ensures that you were listening, and it communicates attentiveness. One partner may begin with, "I felt . . .," and the other partner responds, "I heard you say that you felt . . ." It is rather simple, but it will confirm the message that is being sent and help validate each other's feelings.

Intellectual Intimacy
While emotional intimacy refers to couples sharing their feelings and emotions, intellectual intimacy is about sharing your thoughts, sharing your opinions, learning together, and having thought-provoking discussions. So put down your devices and talk! Talk about your goals and plans for the future, sketch out your dream home together, read a book together, discuss how to create a budget or what debt to pay off next, debate different parenting theories, learn about something that interests you both, deliberate on whom you are going to vote for in the upcoming election, examine your dream jobs, or reminisce about your childhood. Talk about more than just how your day went or what happened at work; truly discuss the bigger things in life.

Experiential Intimacy
There are so many institutions and organizations that compete for our time. Most of us are busy with work, church, school, family, friends, children's sports and activities, and a host of other responsibilities. If we are not careful, we can let all of these other responsibilities and activities encroach on the time couples should be spending with each other. Choose your spouse; choose to spend time creating new and unique experiences together. Many LDS prophets and leaders have suggested weekly dates with your spouse, and not necessarily dates that cost money, but ones that simply include quality time spent together. Find out what each other's interests are (as they do change over time), and discover new hobbies together or have a "usual" eatery or place you love to go; but most importantly, be committed to spending that time with each other. Creating new memories and positive experiences helps couples build a reserve of love that can help them through times of stress and trials.[6]

---
6 *See* Emily C. Orgill, "Date Night—at Home," *Ensign*, April 1991.

Years ago, Elder Joe J. Christensen advised couples, "Make time to do things together—just the two of you. As important as it is to be with the children as a family, you need regular weekly time alone together. Scheduling it will let your children know that you feel that your marriage is so important that you need to nurture it. That takes commitment, planning, and scheduling. It doesn't need to be costly. The time together is the most important element."[7] One of the best ways to nurture a marriage and create experiential intimacy is to continue your courtship throughout your lifespan.

All in all, if someone has the thought, "The only reason my spouse married me is for sex," it is time to have a conversation with your spouse. Open up the lines of communication and discuss what is making you feel that way. Then address the various dynamics and areas of intimacy in your relationship that can be strengthened and more balanced overall. Give your partner the information he or she needs to create change in your relationship. From the Old Testament we read, "Two are better than one; because they have a good reward for their labour. For if they fall, the one will lift up his fellow: but woe to him that is alone when he falleth; for he hath not another to help him up."[8] Remember, marriage is a team sport, and the prizes go to the couples who learn to work together, compromise, and communicate to create and enhance the overall intimacy in their relationship.

---

7   Joe J. Christensen, "Marriage and the Great Plan of Happiness," *Ensign*, May 1995, 64–66.
8   Ecclesiastes 4:9–10.

Question #24:
How does having children change the sexual relationship between husband and wife?

MANY ISSUES WILL ARISE DURING your marriage that may interfere with your romantic life. Jobs, health problems, busy schedules, and children are just a few of those things. Typically, parents report less satisfaction in their marital relationship within the first year after the birth of their first child.[1] Perhaps this is because many new parents are required to navigate additional financial responsibilities, childcare issues, conflicts regarding roles both inside and outside of the home, fatigue from sleepless nights, and other stressors. Even though parenthood has its fair share of challenges, most mothers and fathers believe that being a parent contributes to a meaningful and fulfilling life.[2] Like marriage, parenting is divinely designed to stretch and refine us to become more like our Savior as we learn patience, selflessness, love, compassion, and endurance. Being a parent requires much sacrifice, but it can also be one of life's most enjoyable, satisfying, and rewarding experiences.

Indeed, children may interrupt those times when couples want to be intimate since they are typically attuned to their own needs, not their parents'—at least, until they mature into healthy adults themselves. Moreover, parents may find it difficult to always be sexually spontaneous, especially since their children will be quite spontaneous themselves. Nevertheless, children can bring couples closer

---

1 See B. D. Doss, G. K. Rhoades, S. M. Stanley, & H. J. Markman, "The Effect of the Transition to Parenthood on Relationship Quality: An 8-year Prospective Study," *Journal of Personality and Social Psychology* 96, no. 3 (2009): 601–619, https://doi.org/10.1037/a0013969.

2 See T. Hansen, "Parenthood and Happiness: A Review of Folk Theories Versus Empirical Evidence," *Social Indicators Research* 108 (2012): 29–64, https://doi.org/10.1007/s11205-011-9865-y.

together, especially if the couple adjusts how they cultivate physical intimacy within their marriage despite the challenges children may bring.

Principle

Being flexible and adaptable will help you develop happy and fulfilling relationships with your family. Husbands and wives must "learn to absorb the interruptions of life, and where possible turn them to good account."[3] Couples must learn to go with the flow, especially when it comes to something as unpredictable as children. Things may never go exactly as you had planned or hoped for, especially in matters of physical intimacy.

Almost every married couple with children can attest to being interrupted before or during a sexual experience. While it may be frustrating at the time, it is not the end of the world. Be mindful to avoid viewing your children as "the enemy." Children are not purposely trying to ruin your romantic life—they are just being children. President David O. McKay taught many years ago, "Our most precious possessions, our treasures of eternity, are our children. These merit and should receive our greatest and our most constant care and guidance."[4] Granted, children can certainly hinder their parents' intimate moments; however, not all children are created equal. While some will definitely impede their parents' love life, others may not be as intrusive.

Knowing children can negatively affect a couple's sex life, it is even more important for parents to nurture and show love to their children. If a spouse is harsh with the children or treats them poorly for any reason, there can become a disconnect between partners. Yet, when a spouse treats the children with gentleness, kindness, and patience, those efforts draw a couple closer together. As a result, both men and women are more likely to want to be physically intimate as they experience their spouse positively interacting with the children.

When a child makes it more difficult for physical intimacy or interrupts sex altogether, it is best to resolve the child's needs as best as you can and then try to rekindle your romance. If the flame cannot be revived, then there will be another time and another day to be physically intimate with your spouse. Be patient with yourself, your spouse, and your children. Try to view this challenge with a healthy perspective against the greater purposes of life.

The key to coping with the disappointment is learning how to be flexible and make any needed adjustments to the various situations that may arise. Doug and Dr. Stephen Lamb wrote:

---

3   Richard S. Taylor, *The Disciplined Life: The Mark of Christian Maturity* (1962), 53.
4   David O. McKay, in Conference Report, Oct. 1954, 8–9.

> As soon as you think you've got things figured out, something unexpected happens. A new baby comes along, somebody gets sick, a car breaks down, you don't get the new job, the water heater springs a leak, you're given a calling you don't know anything about, you discover termites, you have a falling out with a friend, you're asked to serve as a room-mother at school, or one of a thousand other things. All these affect your emotional, spiritual, and physical health and influence your desire and ability to be sexually intimate. Finding sexual fulfillment depends on your ability to adapt to the stress of everyday life.[5]

In other words, if it is not the children that interrupt sexual activity, it could be something else. Learning how to effectively handle the unpredictability of marriage and its inevitable disruptions will be important to maintaining connection in the relationship.

Explanation

Most parents have had a variety of experiences in which children have made intimate moments more challenging. Different life stages invite different types of interference. Early in the marriage, pregnancy, delivery, and post-delivery issues can interrupt a couple's sex life. When women are pregnant, sex can often be uncomfortable, or at a minimum, they do not feel very sexy. Once the baby arrives, the sexual relationship between a husband and wife can take a back seat in terms of priorities. Michele Wiener-Davis explained:

> It is completely normal for women to experience a drop in desire following the birth of a baby. The fatigue and physical discomfort following delivery often make sex less appealing. Additionally, prolactin, the hormone that stimulates milk production in nursing women, is known to suppress estrogen and testosterone. A drop in estrogen can cause vaginal dryness, making intercourse uncomfortable. Countless women complain of having low sexual desire, not just immediately following the birth of their children but for years after as well ... Many women say that once they have children, they feel changed. They feel like moms, not sexual beings. Unless a woman understands the

---

5   Stephen E. Lamb & Douglas E. Brinley, *Between Husband and Wife: Gospel Perspectives on Marital Intimacy* (2008), 128–129.

importance of adapting to her changing role as both mother and wife, she may start focusing all of her attention on her children and neglect all aspects of her marital relationship.[6]

As new mothers focus on taking care of their infants, husbands may feel neglected. It is quite common for new fathers to become jealous of the baby who is now getting most of the mother's attention. Husbands should be cognizant of the competing demands on their wives' time, attention, and energy. "If men protest—and they often do—women think them selfish and immerse themselves more completely in their mothering duties."[7] Just as it is important for husbands to be understanding toward their wives' responsibilities and demands as mothers, wives should also try to dedicate some priority time to their husbands and the marital relationship.

When babies become toddlers, they can be disruptive toward romance because they might go to bed late, wake up early, and occasionally cry throughout the night. Sometimes, they will want to crawl into bed with you. Elementary-school-aged children can interrupt intimacy because they are sick or have a bad dream or a host of other factors. High school and college students are often up early for school and activities, and they often stay up late for the same reasons. Their schedules are all over the map, making it difficult for couples to figure out when to try to be alone, much less physically intimate.

Most parents of teens have anticipated evenings when they were hoping for romance, but instead they found themselves helping children with homework projects or picking them up from a late-night activity. Most often, this is how real life works. Things do not always go the way we hope or have planned. Perhaps one of the worst things a husband or wife could do is take out their frustrations on their children—a certain romance killer. It would be better to exercise self-control and patience, laugh together as a couple, and then go pick up your teenager from the movie theater.

Practical Application

Fortunately, there are some things married couples can do to work through the overlapping of their children's needs and their own marital needs:
1. **Embrace the fact that children can be disruptive.** The sooner we accept this concept, the better off we will be! Instead of feeling angry

---

6 Michele Weiner Davis, *The Sex-Starved Marriage: Boosting Your Marriage Libido* (2003), 44, 48.

7 Weiner Davis, *The Sex-Starved Marriage*, 80.

or resentful toward your children, be empathetic and understanding. Show love to your children, tend to their needs, and then regroup with your spouse. If sexual interruptions are occasional occurrences, learn to work with them in mature, Christlike ways. If these disruptions happen more than you feel they should, counsel with each other to find workable solutions.

2. **Consider a plan of scheduled intimacy.** If your spontaneous efforts are often interrupted, consider scheduling your intimate moments together. Many men and women oppose this plan, insisting that their intimate times together should be natural and unplanned. However, remember, there are no guarantees for physical intimacy when you have children in the home. It may be helpful to designate your intimate times together that work for you both. Take turns setting the tone for your intimate times and perhaps initiating sex. If children interrupt your schedule, then you can simply set a new time with each other and try again.

3. **Redefine physical intimacy.** Remember that physical intimacy does not have to focus on sexual intercourse and orgasms alone. Being physically intimate means increasing affection by holding hands, kissing or making out, touching, massaging, and anything that feels pleasurable between partners. Physical affection can build and lead to sex when the timing is right, but just because sex was interrupted, or it did not happen "all the way," doesn't mean there wasn't a connection between a husband and wife. Acknowledge the connection that does take place instead of focusing on what might not have happened.

4. **Get a lock on your bedroom door and set some boundaries.** We are surprised at how many couples regularly let their children sleep in their beds, especially long past the more understandable baby stage. Some couples have reported three to four children in their bed at a time. One couple revealed to one of us that their eighteen-year-old son still sleeps on the floor in their bedroom. This is a big problem for the marital relationship, as the bedroom should be a couple's sanctuary. The bedroom should be a special place for husbands and wives—not necessarily for their children. Dr. Ed Wheat, who specialized in sexual issues, has explained:

> Most important is your need for privacy. In considering buying or building a home, you should pay

close attention to having your bedroom and bath as isolated as possible from other rooms. Every master bedroom needs a good lock, controlled from the inside, of course. Every child should be trained not to disturb his [mom] and [dad] when their bedroom door is locked. If a couple is to concentrate totally on each other (which is necessary for maximum enjoyment), they must be assured of protection from intrusion. Under no circumstances should you allow a child to sleep in the room with you, except perhaps a new baby for the first six months or less.[8]

5. **Practice self-care, and encourage your spouse to do the same.** It's imperative to take care of yourself so that you have the energy to take care of your children *and* each other. Having alone time and time to nurture friendships, as well as maintaining healthy eating, sleep, and exercise habits, can help to provide couples the energy to parent with patience and to foster their physical relationship with each other.
6. **Have a date night regularly.** The practice of having regular date nights is vital for couples to keep their romantic flame alive, especially once children come along. Years ago, Doug used to tell his audiences in his marriage seminars, "Babysitters are cheaper than divorces." Designating a day every week as your date night can do wonders in rejuvenating and enriching your marriage relationship. Find a reliable babysitter and advise them that you are not to be contacted unless there is an emergency. Date night does not have to be anything crazy or extravagant. It can be simply dinner and a movie, going for a walk or drive, or anything that will give a husband and wife alone time to talk and be together without any distractions. It is a great idea to exclude from your date night discussions about distracting topics, such as finances, children, and schedules.
7. **Schedule twenty-four- and forty-eight-hour retreats.** Perhaps twice a year married couples with children need to get away to refuel their relationship as a couple. Children can be demanding on their parents' time and energy. Focused couple time away from all distractions is vital to the health and vitality of the marriage. Invite one of your parents

---

8   Ed Wheat & Gaye Wheat, *Intended for Pleasure*, 4th ed. (2010), 81.

or someone you trust to watch your children for a weekend. You can go to a fancy hotel, rent a cabin, or even just find an inexpensive local getaway. You will discover that when you return home from an overnight getaway, your batteries will be recharged, and you will be a better parent and spouse.

8. **Remember that your marriage comes before the children.** We know it is easier said than done to put your spouse before your children, especially when children's needs tend to be more urgent. However, couples should strive to create a marriage culture of making each other their first priority. Consequently, this will ensure that the relationship will stay healthy and strong as children grow up and leave the home. Husbands and wives should find ways to make each other feel that they are still most important. No one wants to be second fiddle to his or her children in a marriage relationship. Dr. William Doherty once explained:

> I don't hold out my own marriage as a model for all couples. And I don't mean to imply that we had no struggles with our children, or made no mistakes. We had our share of both. But I know we did one thing well: we taught our children that we valued our marriage without devaluing them, that more for us meant more for them, that we were mates before we were parents, and that in the solar system of our family, our marriage was the sun and the children the planets, rather than the other way around.[9]

Find ways to show your children you value your marriage without undervaluing them. Elder Robert D. Hales taught, "By divine commandment, spouses are required to love each other above all others. The Lord clearly declares, 'Thou shalt love thy wife with all thy heart, and shalt cleave unto her and none else' (D&C 42:22)."[10] This also implies that wives should love their husbands with all their hearts and cleave unto them and none else.

Parents should not allow their children to infringe on their sexual lives. There may be interruptions at times, but that is more the exception than the rule. Cultivate a healthy perspective. Remember, children are just doing what

---

9   William J. Doherty & Barbara Carlson, *Putting Family First* (2002), 151.
10 Robert D. Hales, "The Eternal Family," *Ensign*, Nov. 1996, 65.

children do and are ultimately a great joy—even if they stretch us a little. As lovers transition to becoming parents, they can be prepared for the numerous changes children bring by making necessary adjustments, even in the bedroom.

Question #25:
What can married couples do to keep their love alive?

We are aware of a man—a marriage and family therapist—who often taught marriage workshops on weekends. On one occasion, he was teaching a group of Latter-day Saint married couples the importance of meeting each other's marital needs. In his presentation, he said, "Look, meeting your spouse's needs is relatively easy. My wife is sitting here on the front row. I will tell all of you what her needs are right now." This man then rattled off several of his wife's needs, which included things like affection, time together, and the need to feel cherished. After sharing some of these needs with the audience, the man was ready to explain how easy it is to come to know the needs of your spouse. However, before he could say much more and explain how wonderful he was, his wife raised her hand. He was reluctant to call on her, but he mustered up his courage and asked, "Honey, did you want to say something?" She said, "Yes, as a matter of fact, I would love to. You just rattled off four or five of my needs in our marriage. My question to you is, 'When do I get these?'" Wow! You could have heard a pin drop. The room went from laughter and fun to stone-cold silence. The man then explained to the audience that he had some work to do in his marriage, which we all do. But that was a difficult place and time to learn that he was not the awesome marriage partner he thought he was.

Each one of us could improve as a spouse. No matter how wonderful we think we are as a spouse, there is always something we can do better! One of the challenges of married life is putting in the effort to preserve the relationship and working to improve it each day. Many Church leaders, both men and women, have expressed concern about couples getting married in the temple and thinking the hardest part is over when, in reality, the work is just beginning. President Spencer W. Kimball stated, "Many couples permit their marriages to become stale and their love to grow cold like old bread or worn-out jokes or cold gravy."[1] Keeping a marriage alive takes constant attention and nurturing, as well as an awareness of the physical aspect of the relationship. President Harold B. Lee declared, "The most dangerous thing that can happen between you and your wife or between me and my wife is apathy—not hate, but for them to feel that we are not interested in their affairs, that we are not expressing our love and showing our affection in countless ways. Women, to be happy, have to be loved and so do men."[2]

Principle

"A marriage that does not provide nurturance and restorative comfort can die of emotional malnutrition."[3] Sometimes, after couples have been married a while, they can settle into a routine and often begin to take each other for granted. Couples can become less inclined to laugh together, participate in fun activities with each other, spend time together, and engage in deep and meaningful conversations. In short, they have stopped doing all the enjoyable things they once did to fall in love in the first place!

Over time, a marriage that is not fed with time, love, and nurturance will erode, deteriorate, and fail. President Spencer W. Kimball taught,

> Love is like a flower, and, like the body, it needs constant feeding. The mortal body would soon be emaciated and die if there were not frequent feedings. The tender flower would wither and die without food and water. And so love, also, cannot be expected to last forever unless it is continually fed with portions of love, the manifestation of esteem and admiration, the expressions of gratitude, and the consideration of unselfishness.[4]

Therefore, if couples want their marriages to thrive, they will need to invest time, effort, energy, and resources into the relationship.

Explanation

Michele Weiner Davis argues that the most significant contributor to the breakdown of marriages today is the lack of time spent together.[5] Therefore,

---

1 Spencer W. Kimball, *Marriage and Divorce* (1976), 23.
2 *Teachings of Harold B. Lee*, 241.
3 Sandra Blakeslee & Judith S. Wallerstein, *The Good Marriage: How and Why Love Lasts* (1995), 240.
4 Spencer W. Kimball, *Marriage and Divorce*, 22–23.
5 *See* Michele Weiner Davis, *Divorce Busting* (1992).

it is essential that married couples spend quality time together and prioritize each other. Unfortunately, it might be an easy concept to identify and even discuss but much more difficult for a couple to execute as time passes on. Husbands and wives have become busier with education, work, children, church duties, extended family, and other significant responsibilities and distractions. Often, our marital relationships take a hit as we give priority to everything else on our schedules.

Furthermore, our culture is no longer "marriage friendly," and to have a strong marriage can be an uphill battle. Today, being hyper-busy is the new status symbol, and the prizes no longer go to the wealthiest, but the busiest. In fact, we often feel bad if we have free time. Often, we go about searching to fill that time with things to do simply to feel productive. If parents' weekends are not filled with children's sporting events, or their weeknights are not filled with chauffeuring duties, then they somehow feel their kids are missing out. These families are obviously not busy enough! In addition, social media perpetuates the need to stay busy by constantly viewing what other people are doing. Therefore, couples will need to be intentional, giving priority and attention to each other if they want their marriages to survive, let alone thrive. Put each other first, set boundaries for your family, and then schedule time together and make it count.

Practical Application

Couples who report more fulfilling and satisfying marital relationships work at it. Here are fifteen ideas that can help keep your marriage alive and thriving:

1. **Pray together.** Praying *for* each other and praying *with* each other is one of the first steps to strengthening and fortifying your marriage. A recent study conducted at Florida State's Family Institute reported that praying for a spouse could lead to "increased relationship satisfaction, greater trust, cooperation, forgiveness, and marital commitment."[6] For years, apostles and prophets have taught us the importance of couple prayer. For example, President Gordon B. Hinckley declared, "I know of no single practice that will have a more salutary effect upon your lives than the practice of kneeling together as you begin and close

---

6 *See* Danielle Christensen, "Recent Study Confirms LDS Leaders' Teachings That Prayers Strengthen Marriage," *Deseret News* (Aug. 7, 2017), https://www.deseret.com/2017/8/7/20617144/recent-study-findings-support-lds-leaders-teachings-that-prayers-strengthen-marriage.

each day. Somehow the little storms that seem to afflict every marriage are dissipated when, kneeling before the Lord, you thank Him for one another, in the presence of one another, and then together invoke his blessings upon your lives, your home, and your dreams."[7] We know that there is great power in praying together, keeping covenants, and seeking to develop Christlike attributes. Furthermore, when couples seek for the Spirit in their lives, they will receive divine guidance, peace, and spiritual strength.

2. **Keep the commandments and keep your covenants.** There are many ways to seek the Spirit and strive for personal righteousness in your marriage. Prayer, scripture study, church attendance, and temple worship are the staples of gospel-centered living. President Spencer W. Kimball taught,

> To be really happy in marriage, one must have a continued faithful observance of the commandments of the Lord. No one, single or married, was every sublimely happy unless he was righteous. . . . If two people love the Lord more than their own lives and then love each other more than their own lives, working together in total harmony with the gospel program as their basic structure, they are sure to have this great happiness. When a husband and wife go together frequently to the holy temple, kneel in prayer together in their home with their family, go hand in hand to their religious meetings, keep their lives wholly chaste, mentally and physically . . . and both are working together for the upbuilding of the kingdom of God, then happiness is at its pinnacle.[8]

3. **Engage in positive conversations.** Communication is a critical element of a strong, stable marriage. Sharing personal feelings and experiences in depth with each other can help to ease marital challenges. In addition, it is important to include each other in making important decisions. Ask for your partner's opinion, whether regarding a

---

7 Gordon B. Hinckley, *Ensign*, April 1971, 72.
8 Spencer W. Kimball, *Marriage and Divorce*, 24.

financial purchase or what restaurant to go to for dinner. Making decisions together helps improve collaboration and closeness. President Howard W. Hunter explained, "A man should always speak to his wife lovingly and kindly, treating her with utmost respect. Marriage is like a tender flower, brethren, and must be nourished constantly with expressions of love and affection."[9] Couples need time to talk about a wide variety of marital issues that include their relationship, family planning, careers, finances, physical intimacy, and many other things. The critical point is that you both must feel comfortable exchanging thoughts and feelings without fear of criticism, without being put down for your ideas, and without feeling controlled or smothered.

4. **Express affection often.** We all have a need to feel loved and cherished and to be touched. Several years ago, Doug wrote in the *Ensign* magazine, "Physical embraces, hugging, kissing, holding hands, caring for each other, and seeing to each other's needs can help spouses show and feel affection that is crucial for married couples."[10] Kind expressions of love and compassion through touch release a hormone called oxytocin, which reduces stress. In addition, touch has been found to reduce pain and feelings of social isolation.[11] Within our experience of counseling couples, often a husband or wife will label themselves as, "not an affectionate person." This could be a result of past trauma, or most likely, it's due to how their family of origin expressed love and affection. However, it is crucial to a couple's marriage that both partners put forth effort in expressing love through touch and help in breaking the cycle of touch-starved relationships.

5. **Say, "I love you."** As with expressing feelings of love through touch, you can express love to your partner with your words. Florida International University psychologist Lisa Arango says that couples are looking for emotional presence in their spouse. She specifically notes that telling someone you love them is the oxygen for the relationship, keeping it fed and alive.[12] So, tell each other, "I love you," often,

---

9   Howard W. Hunter, in Conference Report, Oct. 1994, 68.
10 Douglas E. Brinley, "What Happily Married Couples Do," *Ensign* or *Liahona*, Jan. 2012.
11 *See* Mariana Von Mohr, Louise P. Kirsh, and Aikaterini Fotopoulou, *Scientific Reports* (Oct, 18, 2017), https://www.nature.com/articles/s41598-017-13355-7.pdf.
12 *See* Gisela Valencia, "Why You Should Say 'I Love You' Today—and Always," *Florida International University News* (Feb. 14, 2020), https://news.fiu.edu/2020/why-you-should-say-i-love-you-today-and-every-day.

compliment each other, tell your spouse how attractive or beautiful they are, express gratitude by saying thank you, and voice what you appreciate about each other. Not only do husbands and wives need to be shown love through actions, but they need to hear love verbally expressed too.

6. **Laugh together.** Having a fun time, enjoying each other's company, and laughing together are crucial ingredients to keeping your love alive. An age-old saying, *Laughter is the best medicine*, comes from Proverbs 17:22, which reads, "A merry heart doeth good like a medicine." In addition, modern research supports the benefits of laughter in relationships. Laughter strengthens the bond between partners, enhances a person's mood, reduces stress and anxiety, increases attraction, boots immune systems, improves relaxation, helps with conflict resolution, fortifies resiliency, and increases marital satisfaction.[13] Marriage expert Judith S. Wallerstein explained that to create a happy marriage, couples need to "share laughter and humor and to keep interest alive in the relationship. A good marriage is alternatively playful and serious, sometimes flirtatious, sometimes difficult and cranky, but always full of life."[14]

7. **Be each other's best friend.** John Gottman, a renowned marriage researcher who has spent decades studying divorce, and author of *The Seven Principles for Making Marriage Work*, has written that friendship is the core of a strong marriage, and it creates happier marriages. Friendship consists of knowing your partner well, their likes and dislikes, their hopes and dreams, and Gottman refers to it as a "love map." Typically, we know everything about our partner in the beginning of our relationship, but knowing your partner is essential throughout the years of your marriage. Be curious about your spouse, learn to ask questions and listen, be each other's cheerleaders, check in throughout the day, and most importantly, be a transparent and trustworthy friend.

8. **Stay healthy mentally and physically.** Once couples are married, they risk getting too comfortable and may focus heavily on work, educational pursuits, or other distractions instead of focusing on

---

13 *See* Lawrence Robinson, Melinda Smith, and Jeanne Segal, "Laughter Is the Best Medicine," *HelpGuide* (July 2021), https://www.helpguide.org/articles/mental-health/laughter-is-the-best-medicine.htm.

14 Judith S. Wallerstein & Sandra Blakeslee, *The Good Marriage: How and Why Love Lasts* (1995), 332.

each other or even on themselves. It is important to continue to exercise, get an adequate amount of sleep, and eat nutritional foods to maintain a healthy body, both physically and mentally. Husbands and wives should strive to feel good about themselves inside and out. Here are a few ideas: stay active, engage in hobbies outdoors as well as indoors, join a gym and work out together, go on long walks and hikes, purchase bikes and go for regular rides, get a new pair of glasses that give you a new look, buy each other some new clothes for date nights or events, and take pride in staying healthy so that you can enjoy your marriage for many years to come.

9. **Cultivate Christlike attributes in your personality and character.** Kindness, charity, love, patience, and selflessness are all qualities of the Savior that we should be seeking to emulate and incorporate in our marriages. As you both work on becoming more Christlike, you will experience more happiness and fulfillment in your marriage. Love each other, serve each other, build one another up, and forgive each other.

10. **Date frequently.** Regular dating will keep a marriage relationship alive and growing. Dates do not have to be expensive or extravagant. You and your spouse need time away from regular routines to renew your friendship and companionship. New perspectives come with time away from the daily grind. That means dating as a married couple is essential to your mental health and outlook on life. Elder Joe J. Christensen reminded us, "Make time to do things together—just the two of you. As important as it is to be with the children as a family, you need regular weekly time alone together. Scheduling it will let your children know that you feel that your marriage is so important that you need to nurture it. That takes commitment, planning, and scheduling. It doesn't need to be costly. The time together is the most important element."[15] Remember, babysitters are cheaper than divorces!

11. **Create rituals together.** Establishing new traditions for your married life helps to strengthen your bond. Whether it's daily rituals, like the way you kiss each other when you wake up in the morning, or weekly rituals, like date night or enjoying family dinners on Sundays, rituals of connection build shared meaning and security in relationships.

12. **Positive sexual relationship.** BYU family scholars Stahmann, Grover, and Young have written, "Studies show that a positive sexual relationship

---

15 Joe J. Christensen, "Marriage and the Great Plan of Happiness," *Ensign*, May 1995, 64–66.

between a husband and wife increases their attraction for each other, stimulates greater energy, and promotes better health. Additionally (as Paul noted in the scriptures), a strong sexual bond between a husband and wife is a powerful resource for resisting temptation. In short, a loving and enjoyable sexual relationship is God's special reward to those who work hard to make the expression of physical love a priority in their lives."[16] The key here is a *loving and enjoyable* sexual relationship, not one that is forced or required. Reading this book alone demonstrates that you and your spouse are interested in creating a positive sexual relationship in your marriage. Strive to learn what will help you and your spouse specifically, put it into practice, and continue to work on this aspect of your relationship to keep the love alive throughout your marriage.

13. **Treat children with kindness.** Be kind to children. A wife may have a difficult time showing affection toward her husband if he mistreats or is unkind to their children. Likewise, a husband will also struggle expressing love to a wife who is harsh, negative, or critical toward their children. When husbands and wives treat each of their children with love, kindness, tenderness, and respect, the marriage is fortified and strengthened, and that love and admiration pours over into the marriage relationship. Men and women can find each other irresistible when they are kind and compassionate parents.

14. **Consider the twenty-four- and forty-eight-hour retreat.** Husbands and wives both need to be rejuvenated. The late LDS psychologist Victor Cline has written, "Every couple needs periodic breaks from the acute stress of everyday living to strengthen their love, improve communication, plan for the future, and renew their marriage vows."[17] Go to a hotel for a night or a resort for a weekend. Better yet, go on a cruise together for about a week. Getting away from the children can benefit both parties. "While food and shelter sustain life, romantic recharging of the relationship is required to sustain the marriage."[18] Occasionally, children need a break from their parents, just as much as parents need a break from them. Getting away, even for a short period

---

16 R. F. Stahmann, W. R. Young, & J. G. Grover, *Becoming One: Intimacy in Marriage* (2004), 12.

17 Victor B. Cline, *How to Make a Good Marriage Great: Ten Keys to a Joyous Relationship* (1987), 196.

18 Stahmann, Young, & Grover, *Becoming One: Intimacy in Marriage*, 109.

of time, can be renewing and refreshing for a couple. Couples should consider getting away at least once or twice a year. This is a wonderful time for couples to renew their love, their relationship, and remind each other why they got married in the first place and why they love and admire each other. In addition, do not forget that it is okay to go away by yourself as well. Go on those girls' trip or guys' trips, and allow your partner time away to truly recharge. Time apart can help you appreciate your spouse even more.

15. **Read a marriage book together or go to counseling together.** Reading and studying how to have a good marriage together is certainly a preventive maintenance program. Couples who take a proactive approach by reading books and talking about ways to improve their marriage will prevent a multitude of problems. If you need additional support as a couple, do not hesitate to reach out to a professional counselor. There is no shame in getting help; rather, it is more harmful when couples let pride impede them from working with someone who could truly provide empathy, comfort, and hope to your marriage. Licensed therapists can assist you and your spouse with conflict resolution, improve communication skills, and establish a stronger connection between partners. If finances are an issue, please reach out to your bishop, as each of us has worked with Church leadership to provide couples with access to much-needed counseling services.

Perhaps the wisest counsel came from President Gordon B. Hinckley, who shared this important key to a great marriage: "A happy marriage is not so much a matter of romance as it is an anxious concern for the comfort and well-being of one's companion."[19] Maybe to have a happy marriage, it is just that simple.

---

19 Gordon B. Hinckley, "What God Hath Joined Together," *Ensign*, May 1991, 73.

Conclusion

WE HAVE ATTEMPTED TO ANSWER these twenty-five heartfelt questions with faith, hope, and optimism. Our desire has been to help you feel better prepared for the honeymoon and the sexual relationship in marriage. We have used gospel principles, scriptures, words of living prophets, and our own best clinical and practical counsel. We know that our Heavenly Father wants you to not only have an eternal marriage, but also a relationship that you enjoy, including the intimate parts of your relationship.

Great strength will come into your relationship and your marriage as you apply the principles in this book. We believe something that President Howard W. Hunter taught years ago. He said, "Please remember one thing. If our [marriages] . . . are centered upon Jesus Christ . . . nothing can ever go permanently wrong. On the other hand, if our lives are not centered on the Savior and his teachings, no other success can ever be permanently right."[20]

May God bless you in your efforts to be more prepared for the intimate sexual relationship in marriage as you turn to your loving Heavenly Father for help in creating the marriage relationship you have dreamed of and desired. We wish you the very best!

---

20 Howard W. Hunter, "Fear Not, Little Flock" (devotional and fireside speech given at Brigham Young University, 1989), 112.

About the Authors

Mark D. Ogletree

Mark is a professional educator, having taught for over twenty years in the Church's seminary and institute program. Since 2010, he has worked as an associate professor in the Department of Church History and Doctrine at Brigham Young University. Mark is the author of books and articles on topics related to marriage, family, mental health, and contemporary Church history. He has also presented at workshops and academic conferences both nationally and internationally. He and his wife, Janie, reside in Provo, Utah. They are the parents of eight children and twenty-four grandchildren. Mark and Janie, are the hosts of a weekly podcast, *Preserving Families*, that focuses on marriage, family, and mental health issues.

Kinsey D. Pistorius

Kinsey is a private practitioner specializing in therapy for female adolescents, women's issues, distressed couples and families, parent-child relationships, young adults, and sexual abuse/trauma. She was born and raised in Houston, Texas, attended the University of Texas at Austin, where she received a bachelor's degree in psychology and sociology, earned her master's degree in marriage and family therapy from the University of Houston, Clear Lake, and her doctorate degree in marriage and family therapy from Brigham Young University. Kinsey worked for the Children's Assessment Center in Houston providing therapy for sexually abused children and their families, she worked for LDS Family Services while earning her doctorate degree, and she supervised graduate-level therapists at the Council on Alcohol and Drugs Houston. Kinsey previously conducted a private practice in Houston but moved her work to the Dallas area in 2012, where she resides with her husband and six children.

Douglas E. Brinley

Doug received his PhD from BYU in family studies in 1975 and then taught at the Institute at Weber State University for twelve years until he and Geri were called to preside over the Texas Dallas Mission from 1987 to 1990. He was hired to teach at BYU in the Department of Church History and Doctrine from 1990 until his retirement in 2009. He has authored, coauthored, or edited sixteen books, fifteen of which are on marriage and family topics. A few include *Between Husband & Wife: Gospel Perspectives on Marital Intimacy*, *First Comes Love* and its sequel *Then Comes Marriage*, and *Living a Covenant Marriage*. His recent books are: *Marital Therapy* and *What We Wish We'd Known before Our Honeymoon*. He spoke on the Know Your Religion circuit for three decades and at BYU Education Week for over thirty years.